LIGHT FROM THE EAST

LIGHT FROM THE EAST
A GATHERING OF ASIAN WISDOM

FRANK MACHOVEC

Stone Bridge Press ◆ *Berkeley, California*

PUBLISHED BY
Stone Bridge Press
P.O. Box 8208
Berkeley, CA 94707
TEL 510-524-8732 • sbp@stonebridge.com • www.stonebridge.com

Front-cover image by Pieter Weltevrede, used by permission of
Sanatan Society, www.sanatansociety.com.

Cover and text design by Linda Ronan.

Printed in the United States of America.

2010 2009 2008 2007 2006 2005   10 9 8 7 6 5 4 3 2 1

LIBRARY OF CONGRESS CATALOGING-IN-PUBLICATION DATA
MacHovec, Frank J.
  Light from the East : a gathering of Asian wisdom / Frank MacHovec.
   p. cm.
  Includes bibliographical references (p.   ) and index.
  ISBN-13: 978-1-880656-98-3 (ISBN-10: 1-880656-98-1)
  1. Asia--Religion. I. Title.

BL1033.M33 2005
200'.95--dc22
                                                      2005024649

 # Contents

To sit alone with a book spread before you in intimate conversation with unseen generations is a pleasure beyond compare.
Yoshida Kenko, CE 1283–1350

�֎ | Introduction

This book began with a Marine during the Korean War who wanted to understand the enemy he might face. That enemy would have been Chinese or North Korean, his age, and likely a Buddhist. The young Marine's study uncovered a rich source of spiritual light from the East. It motivated him to continue to read and reflect on Eastern philosophies for the next fifty years. Bachelor's, master's, and doctoral degrees in psychology deepened his understanding of the value of the light from the East, the wisdom of Asia. Thirty years of daily experience in mental health clinics and hospitals and in private practice enabled him to apply this wisdom to help others find meaning in their lives.

Today, wars over religious and philosophical differences continue, as they have throughout history. The events of 9/11 and other terrorist acts by religious extremists are but the most recent examples. The United Nations and major religions speak of universal brotherhood, yet hate and violence erupt worldwide: between Hindu and Muslim in the Kashmir, Catholic and Protestant in Northern Ireland, Christian and Muslim in Kosovo, and Muslim and Jew in Jerusalem. One nation's freedom fighter is another's martyr and hero. It is unrealistic to expect that one culture or religion can ever dominate the world.

Some fear that these wars will continue. The United States

was founded after a war of revolution. Every generation has fought a war to defend its freedom. In the Crusades, Christianity and Islam wrestled for centuries over the "Holy Land" both considered sacred. In his 1889 "Ballad of East and West" Rudyard Kipling wrote: "East is East and West is West and never the twain shall meet." That's a popular line, but omitted is what Kipling added: "But there is neither East nor West, Border, nor Breed, nor Birth, / When two strong men stand face to face, / tho' they come from the ends of the earth!" That higher principle is what the world has sadly lacked and continues to lack. There is much wisdom in the East, waiting for the world to rediscover and, we hope, apply.

Eastern philosophies are much older than those in the West. Their teachings were chanted before writing systems were even devised. There has never been a war in the name of Buddhism or Taoism. With such an impressive record it makes sense to study Eastern philosophies more closely and apply them to current problems.

Eastern philosophies have excelled in character building. Most of what they teach does not contradict or interfere with any religion. Practicing yoga, studying Buddha's Noble Truths and Eight-fold Path, and reflecting on Zen koans—all are non-denominational. In fact, an atheist can be a Buddhist, *yogi*, or Zen master. The Asian philosophies described in this book contain more of what today are considered valid psychological concepts than do most of the world's religions.

Light from the East is the culmination of fifty years of thought and study. In the Eastern sense, those fifty years are only the preface to the greater lesson of life itself. The Marine who prepared for war became a psychologist to bring peace to troubled minds. This book is a mirror (*roshi*) reflecting the wisdom earned and learned from the light from the East. Though carefully researched, it may nevertheless be criticized by scholars, since criticizing is what scholars do. Readers should know there are no originals of ancient writings, only copies of copies. It is not possible to know exactly what was said or written thousands of years ago or how it translates into modern language. Scholars and reviewers are lumpers or splitters, simplifiers or complicators. I choose to be among the former, striving for meaning over mechanics, the whole more than the parts.

It is hoped that with this book you will experience light from the East. As you will see, it is multifaceted, and, like a fine diamond, each facet or source radiates the same pure light. The first light source is the teaching of Buddha, his Four Noble Truths and Eight-fold Path. Next are the lights of Zen, Lao Tse's *Book of Tao*, the *I Ching*, and yoga. From China, the *Analects* of K'ung Fu Tse and T'ai Chi radiate their lights. From Japan there is Shinto, Kakuan's Bull, Musashi's *Five Rings*, and haiku poetry. *The Tibetan Book of the Dead* completes the multifaceted diamond of Asian enlightenment. The book ends with suggestions for developing meditative awareness to more fully experience the wisdom of the East.

The goal of *Light from the East* is to present the wisdom of Asia without bias, not to convert or persuade but to allow the light to shine of and by itself. I made every effort to stay out of the way of and not distort that pure, natural light. Every available version of ancient writings was used, in an effort to discern what was most likely the original intent. After you have read this book you will be able to see how similar Eastern philosophies and religions are, that there is in fact one light from the East.

Special thanks to Elizabeth Floyd for her superb editing

and excellent suggestions, to Linda Ronan for the cover design, and to Peter Goodman for his commitment to accept this book, thus bringing it to life. The legends and stories have been passed down over generations and it has not been possible to cite original sources. Many have been gleaned from publications of the Buddhist Publication Society, Sri Lanka. They, with the author's translations of ancient writings, are worthy of acknowledgment as "light from the East" and a beacon for the world toward the higher consciousness that Asians know as enlightenment.

F. M.

Light from the East

Truth is one, though sages speak of it by many names.
Rig Veda, 10th century BCE

Words of truth and wisdom stand by themselves regardless of who speaks or writes them. They are true across time, language, and culture. The important religious and philosophical texts of the world offer similar insight and wisdom in moral values, inspiring regardless of their source. However, there is a difference between traditional Western and Eastern approaches to spiritual truth.

EAST AND WEST COMPARED

The West tends to be more social and group-oriented, using shared experiences such as hymn singing, praying, rituals, and listening to sermons to improve moral behavior. The East uses a more personal focus on meditation and individual concentration to improve insight and build character. Critics of the Eastern approach have viewed it as less socially responsible. Critics of the Western approach have seen it as more materialistic and less deep. Here is a tabular comparison of the two:

East	West
slow-paced	fast-paced
more silent	more vocal
reflective	reactive
more passive	more active
internally focused	externally focused
intuitive	concrete
conserving	consuming

Which is best? The West might answer: "Let's test!" A typical Eastern reply might be: "Neither" or "Why is it important to know?" If there is a message from the long sweep of human experience across time it might be: "Neither and both." Science and technology can refine religion and spirituality by testing and refining truth. Religion and spirituality can enrich science and technology by serving as a moral compass, so that science ennobles us and does not demean all that is human.

As the West ventured forth and explored the earth and outer space, the East remained in one place and explored inner space. An appropriate symbol of the West is an astronaut; for the East it is a person seated in quiet meditation. Fast-food drive-through restaurants symbolize the restless impatience of the West; the unhurried Japanese tea ceremony represents the quiet contemplation of the East. The West pushes the river. The East serenely accepts its natural flow and beauty.

With more efficient travel and cultural and technological exchange, East and West may increasingly blend together over time. For better and for worse, there are Western fast-food and fashion outlets throughout the East, and Japanese and Korean cars, yoga and Tai Chi, and restaurants serving Eastern foods throughout the West.

Western theologian-philosopher Paul Tillich was critical of Western religion. In a June 1958 *Saturday Evening Post* article titled "The Lost Dimension in Religion" he commented: "Western religion has become a non-religion and the first step was made by religion itself." He explained: "It had already lost the battle when it defended great symbols not as symbols but as literal stories."

The literalist approach is typical of Western religion. It has caused much conflict and the formation of countless variations in denominations, each believing it alone possesses the purest spiritual truth. Eastern religion differs markedly and may at first seem abstract and mystic, due to its focus on individual development.

In his 1925 book *Science and the Modern World* Alfred North Whitehead wrote: "Christianity always has been religion seeking metaphysics. Buddhism is metaphysics that generated a religion. Buddhism is the most classical example in history of applied metaphysics." Personality theorists from the West, most notably Alexander, Binswanger, Boss, Bucke, Fromm, Goleman, Jung, Maslow, Murphy, Ornstein, Perls, and Tart, reported being influenced by Eastern philosophies.

"ORIENTATION"

Orientation is a word with several meanings. It can refer to adapting to a new job or assignment or adjusting to a new idea. It is used when locating yourself on a map or in a building or other place. In ancient times "the Orient" was a term for lands and people east of the Mediterranean. This book is "oriented" to Eastern thought. By reading it you are being oriented to it.

Multiple and hidden meanings are part of mystic thought and are crucial to Eastern religions and philosophies. When asked to define truth it is said that Buddha sat in silence and raised a beautiful flower high above his head. Another legend tells of Buddha answering the same question by describing a diamond as an example. Truth shines from every facet depending on the intensity and direction of light and the beholder's position relative to it. Absolute truth would be the diamond in its entirety with all its aspects. Each definition that Buddha gave was true and emphasized sensory experience, but he never presented any one answer as being the complete truth. This book reflects a facet of truth as expressed in the Eastern approach, "the light of Asia."

ENLIGHTENMENT

Light is a natural phenomenon. There is sunlight and moonlight. Making a fire and learning when and how to use it was a significant step forward in human history. Light has been a symbol of knowledge and wisdom as well, and is frequently referred to in Judeo-Christian scripture. The opening passage of Genesis describes the creation of the universe when God said: "Let there be light." In mystic thought light is used to signify spiritual enlightenment. Psalm 119 reads, "Your word is a lamp to light my path, without which I would grope in the darkness." In the New Testament, the Gospel of John quotes Jesus as saying, "I am the light of the world" (8:12). In Romans 13:12 Paul says, "Let us put aside the deeds of darkness and put on the armor of light." In Matthew 5:14 Jesus tells his disciples, "Let your light shine before men that they may see your good works and praise your father who is in heaven."

Other ancient civilizations also used light to symbolize truth and wisdom. The Egyptians believed the highest god came from or literally was the sun. The Persian *Zend Avesta* referred to forces of good and evil as those of light and darkness; Ahura Mazda led the forces of light and Ahriman led the dark forces. The Essenes, a Jewish communal group thought to have written the Dead Sea Scrolls, also referred to the forces of light and darkness. At his trial in ancient Athens, Socrates said that he was guided by his own "inner lights." Buddha described his goal in life as seeking enlightenment and his followers refer to him as "the enlightened one." Zen Buddhists seek *satori*, which translates as "a flash of insight."

In every major world religion there have been groups of believers who sought more spiritual light: Gnostic Christians, Hassidic Jews, Sufi Muslims, Sikh and yogic Hindus, Zen Buddhists, and so on. Most see spiritual enlightenment as an individual rather than a group experience, though rituals are often used to stimulate spiritual experience and higher consciousness. For these believers, spiritual truth is more than rituals, teaching, and reading except to the extent that these activities help to realize deeper meaning. Hidden truths are sought beneath the surface of scripture and human interaction. Dylan Thomas described this kind of seeking with the line "Light breaks where no sun shines." Zen Buddhists refer to it as "seeing with a third eye and hearing with a third ear." Mystic light is caught, not taught or thought; it is earned rather than learned.

MYSTICISM

Mysticism seeks a direct link between a person and a higher consciousness or higher power. In Deuteronomy (30:14) Moses hints of it: "The word is very near you; it is in your mouth and in your heart." The goal of mystic thought has many names: mystic unity, the mystic bond, cosmic consciousness. *Yoga* is a word from Sanskrit meaning "to yoke one's self to the universe."

In a 1963 interview, Frank Sinatra was asked about his religious beliefs. He replied: "Religion is a deeply rooted personal thing in which man and God go it alone together without a witch doctor in the middle." In his book *Dynamic Religion*, Henri Bergson wrote: "Religion is crystallization cooled by science, what mysticism pours while hot into the soul" (1932).

Unfortunately, the mystic tie is difficult to perceive. That may be one reason why there are so many religions. Mohandas Gandhi wrote in *Young India*: "God reveals Himself daily to us but we shut our ears to its still small voice" (1921). Some 2,500 years ago, Heraclitus of Ephesus observed: "The Lord who speaks through the oracle at Delphi neither reveals nor conceals but imparts meaning in hints." Such a fragile connection makes misunderstanding more likely.

Regrettably, the history of religion and the world reflect more presumption and rigid orthodoxy than reason and understanding. The result has been religious wars, persecution, and much suffering. Missionaries seek to replace existing belief systems, many much older than their own, presuming theirs to be the only source of religious truth.

It is interesting, therefore, that John Wesley, who founded Methodism, wrote: "My own belief is not the rule for another." Buddha required his followers to say to others when explaining the *dhamma*: "This is what we believe. Whether or not you accept it, peace be with you."

It is in that spirit this book is offered to you. Take from it what is of value to you. It is offered in love, of others and of truth, to provide light and not heat, to enlighten and not inflame.

2
Buddha's Message from the Heart

In many lands and many tongues he [Buddha] gave Asia light that is still beautiful, conquering the world with strong grace.

Edwin Arnold, *Light of Asia* (1892)

SIDDHARTHA

Gautama Siddhartha, who came to be known first as Sakyamuni, sage of the Sakyas, and later as Buddha, was born in about 563 BCE in Kapilavastu near Benares, where India borders Nepal. He was the son of Suddodhana Gautama, chief of the Sakya warrior caste and a man of great wealth and power. Much that has been written about Siddhartha is not verifiable.

It is said a holy man prophesied to Suddodhana that his son would become a great leader. This pleased him, but the holy man then specified that the son's leadership role would be spiritual rather than military. Suddhodhana did not feel a spiritual life was practical or in the family's best interests, so he shielded his young son from anything that might lead to spiritual thought.

As his father wished, Siddhartha married Yasodhara. They had a son, Rahula. Despite his life of luxury and privilege, Siddhartha was not happy. Spiritually sensitive by nature, he reflected on deeper, larger concerns. At age twenty-nine he chanced to see three persons: one very old, another very sick, and one who had just died. He saw that living means getting old, becoming ill, and finally dying. It troubled him that he still did not understand the meaning of life. He met an elderly Hindu holy man who seemed calm and cheerful despite old age and poverty. This so impressed Siddhartha that he left his family and affluence for the life of an ascetic. This event in 533 BCE is known as the Great Renunciation.

For years Siddhartha wandered, searching for the meaning of life. As an ascetic he studied Hinduism from Brahman gurus. He fasted and experienced deprivation, the opposite extreme to his previous affluent life. His fasting brought him near death, but still he found no answers to his deep questioning about the meaning of life. One day, sitting under a bo tree in the town of Gaya in Bihar, the Great Enlightenment came to him. At that moment he became a Buddha. He saw life as based on four truths he called "noble," two of suffering and two of deliverance.

THE WAY TO ENLIGHTENMENT

Thus began the *dhamma* (or *dharma*), the way to enlightenment (*nibbana* or nirvana) that can break the chain of karmic rebirths. Buddha shared it with others for the first time in the Deer Park at Benares. Five monks immediately joined him and followed him through India's Ganges Valley teaching others. Buddhism has been called "the middle way," and in the Hui Neng sermon Buddha referred to his teachings as "the message from the heart." He taught that the search for spiritual truth can begin at any time for anyone: "Your goal can be reached no matter where you turn, right or left. All roads lead upward and you can start anywhere."

Many of Buddha's teachings are as timely today and show remarkable awareness of current psychological concepts. He described "twelve *ayatana*" of sense and perception: the eye for sensing and perceiving form, the ear for sound, the nose for smell, the tongue for taste, the body for touch, and the mind for awareness and imagery.

At the time Buddha taught his middle way Egyptians were mummifying bodies and discarding brains as useless phlegm! Socrates wouldn't be born for another hundred years. Five hundred years before Jesus' Sermon on the Mount, Buddha was teaching the Five Precepts: do no harm to any living thing; offer no false speech; never take what is not given; engage in no sensual excess or misconduct; and use no intoxicants.

Buddhism is as much a philosophy of life and a psychological system of self-help as it is a religion. There are many variations. Hinayana ("Lesser Vehicle") Buddhism—practiced in Burma, Sri Lanka, Thailand, Laos, and Cambodia—follows the Theravada tradition of arahantship, not Buddhahood. Mahayana ("Greater Vehicle") Buddhism is found in Vietnam, Korea, Japan, and China. It emphasizes "insight into emptiness" (*shunyata*) and seeks Buddhahood.

Zen Buddhism evolved from Mahayana as Ch'an in China, and later as Zen in Japan. Vajrayana Buddhism ("diamond vehicle") studies *tantra* (esoteric texts) in India, Nepal, and Tibet, using magic rituals, mystic symbolism, and intricate yogic practices to speed the way to enlightenment.

Despite their variations, all these practices are still recognizable as distinctively Buddhist.

HINDUISM

Buddha was born and raised Hindu, so some knowledge of Hinduism can help us better understand Buddha's ideas (just as one's understanding of Christianity might be enriched by exploring Jesus's Jewish origin). Hinduism is the major religion of India and one of the world's oldest spiritual traditions. Brahma is Hinduism's term for the Creator-god, also called the Supreme Self. He also appears in other forms, such as Atman and Paramatman. His consort is Saraswati, the goddess of knowledge.

Within Brahma there is the Trimurti, a trinity of Brahma the Creator, Vishnu the Preserver and Cosmic Mind, and Shiva the Destroyer and Cosmic Lord. Krishna, quite similar to Christ, is the eighth avatar, or form, of Vishnu. Shiva has a dual identity: Kali or Durga, goddess of death and destruction, and Parvati or Uma, goddess of birth, life, and motherhood. Freud's concept of the eros and thanatos libido— the basic life force to create and procreate and destroy—can be seen in these Hindu archetypes, a word Jung coined to refer to such common elements in human consciousness.

The Hindu trinity has both male and female aspects, which are considered, according to an old Hindu saying, to be "two wings of the same bird." In the *Bhagavad-Gita* (9.17): "I am the father of the universe. I am the mother of the universe.

I am the creator-of-all." Brahma's female counterpart is Saraswati, goddess of knowledge. Lakshmi is Vishnu's consort and goddess of love. All these have male and female forms—with the greater power residing in the feminine—but all are aspects of Brahma.

There are many lesser gods such as Indra of the heavens seen in thunder, lightning, rain, and snow, Agni in fire, Surya in the sun, and Yama in far and unknown countries. Hindus worship many gods and goddesses, some especially revered by villages and families. Buddha departed from this tradition and focused on character development without emphasizing any gods. Because of this some have criticized Buddhism as being atheistic. Hindus do not find many gods confusing or inconsistent. It is said Brahma's many forms are like the water in streams, rivers, lakes, and oceans, and in dew, fog, rain, snow, and ice, all aspects of one thing.

The *Vedas* are Hindu sacred scriptures. According to legend they are more than five thousand years old, chanted long before there was writing. The *Vedas* are poems, prayers, rituals, hymns, and chants that include the mystic-philosophical *Upanishads*. Hindu literature is extensive. The *Bhagavad-Gita* is a dialog between the god Krishna and the warrior Arjuna. *Puranas* are legends of Hindu heros and heroines, gods and goddesses, and contain the Hindu version of creation. *Ramayana* is the story of good Prince Rama and the demon Ravana. *Manu Smriti* describes and justifies the caste system (now illegal in India, but much social bias still exists).

The *Mahabharata* is a collection of stories of good and evil. There are six major branches of Hindu philosophy: *nyaya,* based on logic and reason; *vaisheska,* relying on nature for guidance; *sankhya,* based on creation themes in the *Upanishads; yoga,* physical and spiritual exercises based on the *Upanishads*; *purva-mimansa*, emphasizing rituals; and *vedanta*, focused on the *Bhagavad-Gita*, *Upanishads*, and *Brahma Sutra*. Some Hindu gods were believed to have animal forms. This explains "the sacred cow" and the reverence and care given them.

Hinduism teaches the law of karma, that rebirth is based on conduct in past and present lives. That is the symbolism of the wheel on the flag of India. Buddha differed with the concept of karmic destiny as an endless chain of rebirths based on previous conduct and with the caste system that resulted from it. He agreed on the need for self-control and higher moral behavior and formulated the Four Noble Truths and the Eight-fold Path as a standard of conduct. His approach to developing meditative awareness and a higher consciousness was similar to yoga and used many of the same terms for the stages and meditative states involved.

THE FOUR NOBLE TRUTHS

The Four Noble Truths are the foundation of Buddhism. They are the theory—and the Eight-fold Path stemming from the fourth Truth is the method—for achieving *nibbana*, or enlightenment. There are four signs of *nibbana*: a feeling of freedom; self-realization and insight; a sense of moral purity (in standards, values, integrity, and self respect); and serene contentment that could be described as childlike joy or simply as happiness.

The First Noble Truth: The Wheel (Dukkha)

The first Noble Truth is *dukkha* (the wheel). It is a message of pain, that every living thing must know pain. We are born in pain, we die in pain, and some pain in life is inevitable. The symbol of this truth is a huge revolving wheel, the wheel of destiny on which all living things are impaled and which runs over them. This pain can encompass both the physical and the mental. Buddha described physical pain in terms of birth, illness, hunger, thirst, injury, aging, death, accidents, and catastrophes. He described mental pain as resulting from anger, fear, hate, anxiety, frustration, selfishness, reckless ambition, or excessive sensuality. Psychological pain can come from dissatisfaction, depression, disappointment, discomfort, deprivation, distortion, and delusion (ignorance).

The Second Noble Truth: The Hub (Tanha)

The second Noble Truth is *tanha* (hub of the wheel). The message here is that the source of pain is within you, in what Buddha called craving or selfishness. He warned against "six excesses" that cause suffering: form, sound, smell, flavor, material things, and mind-objects. To overcome them requires eye-based, ear-based, nose-based, tongue-based, body-awareness-based, or mind-based attention specific to the problem source.

Modern research confirms that there is a significant psychological component to physical pain. The longer pain persists the worse it feels because of our frustration and impatience with it. Likewise, the longer psychological distress continues, the deeper and more pervasive it becomes.

The Third Noble Truth: It Need Not Be So (Nirodha)

The third Noble Truth is *nirodha*. The first two truths are negative and pessimistic, but the message of this third truth is *it need not be so;* pain need not be our only reality. The source of suffering and karmic rebirths can be stopped. *Nirodha* is Buddha's promise of Perfect Enlightenment (*nibbana*) for anyone who follows "the way," and it distinguishes Buddhism from Hinduism, which teaches continuous rebirths based on evils done during one's lifetime. Because early Buddhism stressed character development in this life without reference to God or a heaven after death, Hindu critics consider Buddhism to be atheistic. A "western paradise" was added centuries later, probably to compete with Christian missionaries.

The Fourth Noble Truth: The Way Out and Up (Magga)
The fourth and final Noble Truth is *magga*, "the way" of the Eight-fold Path, the eight steps leading to higher awareness and better character. To realize this truth requires earnest study, regular meditation, and diligent practice of Buddhist teachings. The eight steps are a course in character building as timely today as when they were first taught 2,500 years ago. Buddha called the eight steps "the wide path" open to all.

* * *

To summarize: the first two Noble Truths are negative and pessimistic (living is painful; pain is essentially self-inflicted); the last two are positive and optimistic (it need not be so; the Eight-fold Path is the way up and out). This half-dark, half-light pairing can be seen in the interaction of Yin and Yang, the symbol of Taoism to be explored later in this book.

THE EIGHT-FOLD PATH

When describing the Eight-fold Path, Buddha said: "Forging these eight links does not bring honor or fame. It is a chain that does not bind but frees. It frees you from yourself. It frees you from itself." The path is compatible with other religions, and when Buddha explained it to others he always showed respect for his listeners. He taught his followers to begin thus: "Here is The Way. Accept it if you wish and apply it. Decline if you wish, with a blessing upon you. Either way, peace be with you." The eight steps are to be taken in order, with every step resting firmly on the one below. Translations customarily refer to each step as "right," which implies that there is only one right way to achieve each step, but in fact Buddha may have meant simply to suggest a better, or best, way to proceed.

Step 1: Right Understanding

Right or correct understanding, view, or attitude is the "wake-up call" of the fourth Noble Truth opening the door to the Eight-fold Path. It forms the foundation for all that follows. For that reason the foundation should solidly rest on a clear understanding of the Four Noble Truths. Buddha said that failure to follow this step has caused more suffering than any of the others. Completing this step requires right understanding, or right view, of yourself, of others, of truth, of evil and suffering and their causes, and of ultimate reality.

Mastering this step empowers you to see clearly and in depth what is important or trivial, or good or evil, and how thoughts, feelings, words, and actions can help or hinder personal growth and spiritual development.

Step 2: Right Thinking

Step 2 requires seeing what is there and not what you would like to see or are afraid to see. The second step of our Western scientific method is to observe objectively, yet Buddha was teaching this process 2,500 years ago. Mastering this step, of "right thinking," is being able to "see without naming" or labeling, because doing so identifies, classifies, and judges. Right thinking is unobtrusive, letting everyone and everything "be" without personal bias.

Step 2 is like taking a mental shower. It helps you to be mentally clean of bias. In ancient Greece those who entered temples first washed themselves at a nearby spring, in a purification rite. Step 2 helps develop self-control, self-discipline, and a clearer focus on the right thing to do. When you achieve right thinking you are free of prior conditioning and preconceived notions, insulated from hate and cruelty. It transforms the harmful to the harmless. In Buddha's words you become "pure as a gentle breeze."

Step 3: Right Speech and Silence

Achieving this step requires speaking truth kindly, simply, or in silence. If you know nothing, then say nothing. If you have nothing significant to say, be silent. If you cannot say anything good, also remain silent. Do not lie or gossip. Use speech and silence to unify, or join together, not to separate. Use words that simplify and do not complicate or confuse. Speak or be silent to give light, not heat, to help and not hurt. Buddha cautioned against using words as weapons: "Wrong speech hurts and cannot heal."

Buddha described five kinds of wrong speech: glib talk, lies, slander, harsh words, and idle chatter. He gave five descriptions of right speech: modest, sincere, truthful, dependable, consistent. You can be hurt being truthful, as Norman Vincent Peale pointed out: "Twist the truth and make a hit; tell the truth and get hit!" Buddha offered words of comfort when verbally attacked: "As the elephant endures the arrow, so

The
Eight-fold
Path
—
29

should you patiently bear with abuse, for there are many unkind archers in the world."

Step 4: Right Action—Conduct

This step requires that "every action should weaken a fault." It is to seek and enjoy only what you need, to accept humbly and graciously what is given to you. You should not take what is not yours or indulge yourself to excess. The goal is to be kind and gentle to everyone and every living thing. You rejoice in the happiness of others. Whatever you do should be for the good; if you are unable to do good, do nothing. Like Hippocrates' admonition to his students, Buddha stressed "do no harm." This ancient standard is still the standard in litigation over malpractice and negligence.

Buddha warned about "defilements" to be avoided: murder, stealing, lying, slander, ill will, sexual misconduct, useless talk, harsh words, false views, covetousness, and intoxicants. He warned, "there is no fire like lust; passion does not die out, it burns out." Legend has it that Buddha counseled his son Rahula, "as you see your reflection in a mirror, so you should reflect on what you are doing." Achieving Step 4 brings inner peace and an attitude of quiet repose.

Step 5: Right Livelihood

Right livelihood means finding work that satisfies and fulfills because life itself is a mission, not just a career, living is giving, and every day is a challenge, an opportunity to live it as if it were your last. Some day it will be. Achieving Step 5 means learning to be content with what you have, wise in spending, not indebted, and "blessed being blameless." Buddha urged followers to find "pure livelihood" without dealing in lethal weapons, poisons, intoxicants, animals for slaughter, or activities that hurt people. He cautioned against killing, stealing, cheating, dishonesty, and deceit. At the basis of these admonitions was reverence for life, kindness to animals, and the belief that all men, women, and children are members of the same family, the human race.

Step 6: Right Effort

Step 6 requires doing your best wherever you are to continue to grow personally and spiritually. Buddha said: "I know of no other thing of such power to prevent evil as right effort." He described four "great efforts": to avoid craving and ignorance; to overcome craving and ignorance so that they have no hold over you; to develop energy and strength to do good and avoid evil; and to continue your journey along the Eight-fold Path.

These efforts require physical and mental energy: "As weeds are removed before seed is sown, so you should remove unwanted weeds from your mental garden."

Step 7: Right Mindfulness

The goal of Step 7 is mindfulness or heedfulness, an important Buddhist value. Mindfulness is a state of concentration, of awareness and attention, "being with it." It is above and beyond right understanding because it involves active thinking, especially critical judgment. You need to be able to think about what you choose to think and about what is important along the Eight-fold Path to enlightenment. Mindfulness is developed by using it every day in word and action. In time it becomes like a trusted friend always at your side.

Right mindfulness is an individual achievement done alone

in quiet uninterrupted contemplation away from the stress of everyday life. One sign of it is a quick mind. In Buddha's words: "Heedful among the heedless, awake among those asleep, the wise succeed like a fast horse that overtakes a slower one."

Step 8: Right Concentration

Buddha likened this final step to a strand braided, with Steps 6 and 7, into a strong rope. These three steps interact synergistically, in a way that is greater than the sum of the parts. Buddha considered right concentration a mental exercise and stressed developing the mind and character. Buddhist meditation is not intended to transcend existence as in yoga, but focuses more on certain mental processes and how to overcome them. This results in a calm, reflective state of mind "beyond bliss and suffering," when "the mind is pure and radiant as at birth."

Buddha said, "The unwise are half-filled vessels but the wise are deep, calm lakes." There is no trance state or paranormal power in Buddha's Eight-fold Path but either can occur. Buddha described two states of meditation: the "steady mind" (*samatha-bhavana*) of serenity and inner peace, and "insight meditation" (*vipassana-bhavana*), which is the higher consciousness of oneness or mystic unity. "Insight meditation" frees the mind to wander where it will. As the mind wanders it empties itself of needless thoughts and then opens to a higher level of consciousness.

There's an old saying among mountain men: if you're ever lost in a snowstorm, let go of the reins and the horse will take you home. Insight meditation is like that. Zen Buddhists call it "falling off an imaginary log" or "going down the well." Researchers use this method when they let the data "take them where it will," toward a pattern or a conclusion. In ancient times

Zen archers would meditate so that archer, bow, arrow, and target were one. Expert marksmen today do the same, though they may not be aware that Buddha taught the technique 2,500 years ago.

BUDDHA'S LAST WORDS

Buddha's gentle, sincere nature is reflected in his final words. He was in his eighties and had traveled widely, explaining the Four Noble Truths and the Eight-fold Path. As near as we can tell, he died of acute indigestion or unintentional food poisoning from a meal prepared by a devout follower. It is interesting to note the honesty of the account of Buddha's death twenty-five hundred years ago. It is said that hundreds of monks and nuns were with him when he died. They listened carefully, for they knew, as he did, that death was near.

> Be islands unto yourselves. Be a refuge to yourselves.
> > See truth as an island and as a refuge.
> Do not seek a refuge in anyone but yourselves.
> > And whoever, now or after I am gone, is an island and a
> > refuge to themselves, and takes no other refuge, but seeks
> > truth as an island and a refuge, will reach the farther
> > shore, but they must make the effort themselves.
> My age is now full ripe. My life draws to a close.
> > I leave you, I depart, relying on myself alone.
> Be earnest, then, holy, full of careful thought.
> > Be steadfast in resolve; watch over your own hearts.
> > Who wearies not but holds fast to his truth and law shall
> > cross the sea of life and bring an end to grief.
> Do not weep. Do not distress yourselves. Have I not told you
> > it is in the very nature of things we must eventually be
> > parted from all that is near and dear to us? Everything

born, developed, and organized has within itself the
means of its own demise. How then can it be otherwise
that a being should pass away? Nothing else is possible.
It may be some of you will say "the word of the Teacher is no
more and now we are without a leader."
    You must not think this. The Dhamma and Rules I have
given you, let them be your teacher after I am gone.
This I tell you: decay is inherent in all things.
Work out your own salvation, with diligence.

Zen Mind: Insight in Sparks and Flashes

*Do not get entangled with any object
but stand above, move on, and be free.*
Rinzai Zen saying

BODHIDHARMA AND CH'AN / ZEN

The legendary founder of Zen Buddhism is Bodhidharma, the "blue-eyed monk" who journeyed from India to China in CE 520. It may be that references to his "blue eyes" simply marked the dramatic change brought to traditional Buddhism by Zen, or that blue symbolized wisdom.

Known in China as Ch'an (pronounced like "John"), Zen Buddhism flourished during the Sung dynasty (CE 860–1279). Japanese monks studied it in China and brought it in the sixth century to Japan, where it is known as Zen. Eisai founded the Rinzai school in Japan (ca. CE 1100) using riddles and seeming contradiction to gain insight. Dogen (ca. CE 1200) founded the Soto school, based heavily on readings from Mahayana Buddhism.

Both Rinzai and Soto emphasize the importance of meditation. The names *Ch'an* and *Zen* both derive from the Sanskrit word *dhyana* (pronounced "dzhanna"), meaning "meditative mind." Some refer to this as "Buddha mind." Zen is a variation of Buddhism but adds its direct method of insight learning to Buddha's "message from the heart." It is a blend of Mahayana Buddhism and Taoism that studies reality intensely, in order to experience higher consciousness. The Zen mind is described in a saying of the Rinzai school: "Do not get entangled with any object but stand above, move on, and be free."

In many ways Zen is the opposite of Western materialism. The world is seen as it is, without naming or classifying, owning, acting, reacting, or changing it. A Zen master would be shocked at Tennyson's poem that begins, "Flower in the crannied wall, / I pluck you out of the crannies" because it speaks of taking the life of a flower for selfish enjoyment. The Zen way is to leave the flower where it is, within nature, alive, so that its beauty can radiate freely, even if no one else should ever see it.

ZEN PARADOX

The goal is a mind "open as the sky"—so open, in fact, that it becomes "no mind." With typical paradox Zen teaches that to be filled the mind must first be emptied. Traditional learning is not the way. Zen is inductive and intuitive and may sometimes seem anti-intellectual. Zen is caught, not taught, in flashes of instant insight called *satori* (Japanese) or *tun-wu* (Chinese) like a "mystic leap into the unknown" or "falling off an imaginary log."

Zen "no mind" is like a clear pane of glass, or a mirror,

compared to the Western mind. Zen mind sees with a third eye and hears with a third ear, without judging. Western mind must name, classify, and interpret, intensely seeing and hearing—and missing the point! In Zen there is no need to add words to what already is. You already know all you need to know and very likely know too much. Your cup is overflowing. Zen language is direct, sometimes crude or shocking, even profane. Satori can be a gentle nudge, a prod, or a lightning bolt in impact.

"MINDLESS SIMPLICITY"

Zen originated in China, founded by the legendary blue-eyed monk Bodhidharma. After his death a patriarch led the movement. In the seventh century CE, Hung Jen was the fifth patriarch. When it came time to choose the sixth patriarch, he asked his followers to write a few lines that best described Zen. Two finalists emerged. Shen Hsiu, one of the two, wrote this:

> The body is the Bodhi tree;
> The mind is like a clear mirror standing.
> Take care to wipe it all the time;
> Allow no grain of dust to cling to it.

Not bad! There is much Zen in it. Shen Hsiu was a close follower of Hung Jen and was favored by many to succeed him. Hui Neng worked in the kitchen and did not have the standing of Shen Hsiu. His entry was a response to Shen Hsiu's:

> The Bodhi is not like a tree;
> The clear mirror is not standing anywhere.
> Basically there is nothing in existence.
> Where then is there a grain of dust to cling?

The first entry reflects an inductive developmental approach that some have called "mirrorlike purity." The second is intuitive and existential, one of "mindless simplicity." It came as a surprise when Hui Neng was named the sixth patriarch. Shen Hsiu left and founded what has become known as the Northern School. Hui Neng's approach, which became known as the Southern School, prevailed. This approach emphasizes finding and applying Zen to everyday life as much as rituals and meditation though both continued to be practiced.

Hui Neng taught that there is a risk in self-awareness. It can become more selfish than selfless, in a kind of overthinking. This ties one to the earth and interferes with rising upward into a higher consciousness. The Northern School was more structured and relied more on rituals and sitting, standing, and walking meditation. So, like Judaism, Christianity, and Islam, Zen also had its schisms.

KOANS

Koans are insight riddles that can be solved by deductive reasoning or factual knowledge. The best Zen answers never rely on scientific fact or social custom. They aim at meditative awareness, a mystic leap upward with a transformational, transcendent quality. When koans work they give an instant burst of satori, an "Aha!" experience. Satori is best achieved by avoiding intellect, reason, and fact. Here are examples:

STUDENT: What is perfect enlightenment like?
MASTER: Perfect enlightenment is like thieves breaking into a vacant house.

STUDENT: Is it useful to read the sutras (scriptures)?
MASTER: There are no paths, roads, or crossroads. The

mountain is always there, fresh and green all year.

Regardless of your direction you may have a very nice walk.

To achieve enlightenment requires an ultimate "letting go" of connections to material things and possessiveness of any kind, in a free and open search for enlightenment. The Western saying "you can't take it with you" is equally true in Zen, but Zen would add that "there is no reason whatever to want to do so." An enlightened mind is "wide open as the sky" in tune with the universe, a Zen vacant house!

Satori Spark

Koans are used to ignite a spark of satori. One way you yourself can use koans is to type or write each one on an index card. Use one card at a time for self-study; reflect on its meaning and be open to a flash of satori. When you have completed all the cards, use them again as a Zen refresher by randomly drawing a card.

Types of Koans

The following are some examples of the different types of koans commonly studied.

Basic Questions

1. What time is it?

2. When is your birthday?

3. Who is your mother?

4. Who is your teacher?

5. How well can you see?

6. How rich are you?

7. How old are you?

8. What do you own?

9. Where is home?

Comparison

10. Who is the best teacher?

11. What is the best knowledge?

12. Who is your best friend?

13. How can you know the most beautiful?

14. Who is your worst enemy?

Paradox

15. What is the sound of silence?

16. How is failure success?

17. How is loneliness good?

18. How is leaving arriving?

19. How is ugliness beautiful?

20. How is dark light?

21. When is good evil?

22. When are differences the same?

23. How can greatness be small?

24. How is emptiness full?

25. How is ending beginning?

26. When is man not a man and woman not a woman? (When is a man a woman and a woman a man?)

Lessons

27. What is the lesson of emptiness?

28. What is a lesson of uncarved wood?

29. What is a lesson from a seed? a flower?

30. What is a lesson from sunrise and sunset? noon?

31. What is a lesson from water? the ocean? the beach?

32. What is a lesson from the wind? The sky? clouds?

33. What is a lesson from a waterfall?

34. What is a lesson from snow? ice? rain? dew?

35. What is a lesson from fire? from a candle?

36 What is a lesson from an insect? a bird? an animal?

37. What is a lesson from the earth? the sun? the moon?

Contradiction

38. How is a baby your grandparent? Explain. And so?

39. What effect would it have if a rose was called a weed? Explain. And so?

40. How is this a happy message: grandfather dies; father dies; son dies? Explain. And so?

41. Candle, wick, and flame: which is most important? How are these the same? Explain. And so?

42. Why give a lighted candle or lantern to a blind person? Explain. And so?

43. How can you reach higher on tiptoe from the highest mountain? Explain. And so?

44. Two persons argue. Both are right. Neither is right. One is wrong. Both are wrong. They teach each other but fail the lesson. How can all this be? And so?

45. A boat sinks. Does water flow into it or does it lower itself into the water? Which is more powerful? Which wins? Explain. And so?

46. How are black and white the same? How do they need each other? Which is more important? Explain. And so?

47. Hammer hits nail. Which is stronger? How are they similar? How are they different? Which yields more? Which wins? Explain. And so?

48. There is a deadly snake and a piece of rope in a totally dark room with no windows or light. How can you know the snake from the rope? Explain. And so?

49. If you call this a sentence you are trapped by its name. If you don't, you contradict fact. What do you call it? Explain. And so?

50. Zen is nothing. Zen isn't nothing. Zen isn't know—thing. Zen knows. Zen no's. Zen nose. Zen knows nothing. Zen knows no-thing. Zen is something. Zen is anything. What is, is Zen, but Zen isn't it. Zen is, but isn't. How can all this be so? Explain. And so?

51. Half of Zen is nonsense. Half of Zen is good sense. Half of Zen is both. Half of Zen is neither half. How can this be? And so?

52. Is there sound where there is no ear? Explain. And so?

53. What is the sound of one hand clapping? Explain. And so?

54. How do you play the solid iron flute that has no holes? Explain. And so?

PARABLES

Stories and parables demonstrate the Zen approach. Like koans you either "get it" or miss the flash. Here is a sampling:

The Monk's Chair

It was the custom for Buddhist monks to be seated according to seniority. One day a young student used a Zen approach and sat in the chair of the monk who was the oldest and who was considered the most enlightened. The old man walked over to the seated student and started a Zen dialog.

OLD MONK: How old are you in the Buddhist way?
STUDENT: I am as old as the most prehistoric Buddha.

With this remark the dining room became silent. Everyone recognized that the student had presented a very powerful Zen argument. Without hesitation the old monk smiled graciously and calmly replied: "Move over. You are my great grandson."

SPARK OF SATORI: This is typical Zen "one-upmanship" with a deeply spiritual meaning that underlies a seemingly superficial prank. Zen practitioners are cheerful and childlike because of the utter simplicity of the method. They see the world as a baby might—purely, simply, as it is.

The Zen Teacup

A Western scholar visited a famous Zen Master. The scholar described his education and training, his research and publications, travels and interests, then said he wanted to learn about Zen. As he talked on and on, the Zen master served tea. He poured it into the visitor's cup and continued until it overflowed. "Can't you see it's full?" the visitor asked anxiously. "Yes," the master calmly replied, "just as your mind is filled and overflowing with its own ideas. I cannot pour out Zen to you until you bring me an empty cup."

SPARK OF SATORI: Zen is experiential rather than cognitive, practical rather than theoretical. You can learn it but never know it, read it but never realize it. The Zen master demonstrated that personal bias and even previous education can be obstacles to enlightenment.

The Miracles of a Zen Master

A Zen master was sitting in meditation when a Western missionary approached.

MISSIONARY: The founder of my religion made miracles.

He could walk on water. What can you do?
ZEN MASTER: I only do small miracles. When I am
hungry I eat. When I am thirsty I drink. When I am
lonely I think on deeper truths. And when I am insulted
I forgive.

SPARK OF SATORI: This exchange contrasts the direct, impatient
West with the indirect, reflective East.

The Monk's Mission

Centuries ago there was a Buddhist monk in Japan who made
it his life's mission to arrange for Buddhist scriptures to be
printed for the first time in Japanese. He traveled from village to village to raise the money needed. In ten years he had
enough, but the Uji River flooded and there was a great famine.
He used the money to buy rice for the needy.

Again the monk traveled far and wide to raise the money
needed to print Buddhist scriptures in Japanese. After another
ten years he had enough, but this time there was a great plague
and he used the money to buy medicine for the needy.

A third time he traveled from village to village and in ten
years had enough money. Though very old and tired, before
he died the monk saw his life's mission fulfilled. The Buddhist
scriptures were printed in Japanese. You can see them in muse-
ums and libraries today. But it is said by those who really know
that the books he had printed are not as good as his first and
second editions.

SPARK OF SATORI: This parable is somewhat similar to Leigh
Hunt's poem "Abou Ben Adhem." In this poem, an angel appears one night before Ben Adhem, writing "the names of those
who love the Lord" in a book of gold. Ben Adhem asks if his
name is there, and when he is told that it is not, asks the angel:

"I pray then, then, write me as one who loves his fellow men."
The poem ends: "The next night / It came again ... / And
showed the names whom love of God had blessed, / And, lo!
Ben Adhem's name led all the rest." So it was for Tetsugen who,
in helping others, fulfilled a mission as great, perhaps greater,
than that he originally sought.

Heaven and Hell, Up Close!

The Emperor's Captain of the Guard, a famous samurai warrior, retired. He wanted to spend his retirement years seeking
enlightenment, and so he visited a respected Zen master to plan
his studies.

OFFICER: I want to study your philosophy and
meditation.
MASTER: What do you seek to know?
OFFICER: I really want to know if there is a heaven and a
hell.
MASTER: Who are you?
OFFICER: I was Captain of the Emperor's personal guard.
MASTER: Nonsense. What kind of emperor would
tolerate someone like you?
OFFICER (*indignant*): I am a Samurai and have won many
battles.
MASTER: I don't believe it. You look like a beggar to me.
(*The officer rattled his sword, eyes blazing with irritation and anger.*)
MASTER: Oh, I see that you have a sword. You probably
stole it. I doubt you know how to use it. It's probably
rusty and too dull to cut anything anyway.
(*The enraged officer drew his sword and held it with both hands over
the master's head.*)
MASTER (*calmly*): Now you have half the answer. The
gates of hell are now open to you.
(*At first confused, and then exasperated, the officer, whose success on*

the field of battle was due to quick thinking and intelligence, stood frozen from the sudden impact of the master's words, a devastating blast of satori. Trembling, he threw down his sword and fell to his knees, weeping.)

MASTER (calmly): And now, my son, you have the other half of the answer. The gates of heaven are now open to you.

SPARK OF SATORI: Stressful situations are often used to demonstrate Zen principles. The master entered the officer's world of martial arts and used its references to get attention and provoke a situation that he could then use to enable the officer to experience satori.

The Princess's Head

A princess was upset because she could not see her own face, and so she thought she had lost it. Her family reassured her that they could see her face, but she could not accept it. "You're just saying that because you're my family." A mirror was placed before her but she said: "This is just a picture of me. It is a head, but not my head." In desperation her father tied her to a post in the village square with a sign over her head asking all who passed by to reassure her that she had a head. Many people did, but this only made the princess more upset. She lamented: "But I can't see it. I can't feel it. I have no head." An old man walking slowly with the aid of a cane read the sign. Suddenly he swung his cane full circle and struck the princess on the head. She cried out in pain. "That," said the old man, "is your head."

SPARK OF SATORI: This centuries-old parable is an example of the "tough love" approach, or reality therapy. Sometimes a simple act is better than a wordy explanation. Sometimes feelings teach better than thinking. I've used this story as an example of what may be the oldest example of Fritz Perls's gestalt therapy that uses direct confrontation in much the same way. Experiential therapy!

The Monk's Woman

Two Buddhist monks were begging for food in the village, a daily task. It was the rainy season and the streets were muddy. An attractive woman dressed in fine silk stood at the side of the road, afraid to cross. Without hesitation, one of the monks offered to help. She consented and he picked her up and carried her across. The other monk was very upset. All the way back, on the long road to the monastery, he harangued the first monk: "You know very well contact with women is strictly forbidden. We should never go anywhere near a woman, especially such a pretty one dressed in fine silk. And we should certainly not touch one." At the entranceway the first monk smiled graciously and said, "Brother, I put that lady down hours ago, but you're still carrying her."

SPARK OF SATORI: For centuries Zen masters have asked newcomers: "How much baggage do you carry?" Or: "I hope you have not brought too much baggage." It sometimes takes time to dispose of it." These are typical Zen ways of referring to mental unfinished business, unresolved problems, and unsettling ties to the past. Many people have been disappointed on carefully planned vacations because they looked forward to a carefree time only to discover they brought *themselves* along, with all their positive and negative traits. In Zen it is best to "travel light." Only this instant is real. Yesterday is gone forever and tomorrow is not here.

EXISTENTIALISM

One Western philosophy similar to Zen is existentialism, which is usually defined as a philosophy emphasizing the individual as free and self-determining. This philosophy emerged from Europe during and after World War II. One provocative existentialist statement is: You are free; define yourself. While some criticize Nietzsche's provocative statement that "God is dead," in a Zen sense that statement makes us, the living, fully responsible for our own conduct, without any deity who might intervene.

Another example is the idea that "there is no meaning in life," which implies "except that which we bring to it." Existentialists are realistic but also idealistic. Nobel prize winner Jean-Paul Sartre wrote in his 1939 book *Situations*, "We are not the sum of what we have but the totality of what we do not yet have, of what we might have." Karl Jaspers, the German psychiatrist-philosopher, wrote, "When I become aware of myself I see that I am in a world in which I wonder and ask myself what really is."

4 Tao Spirit: Seeing In and Through

Looked for, it cannot be seen; it is invisible.
Listened for, it cannot be heard;
it is inaudible.
Reached for, it cannot be touched;
it is intangible

Lao Tse

THE *BOOK OF TAO*

Taoism (pronounced "Dow-ism") is an ancient Chinese phi-losophy attributed to Lao Tse (pronounced "Louts"), also known as LaoTzu, Lao-tsze, Laozi, and Li Erh (ca. 604–531 BCE). According to legend, he was the keeper of the archives in Honan province during the Chou dynasty and highly regarded for his wisdom. When he was very old he left his work one day and, dressed humbly, rode a black ox into the mountains to die.

A guard at the frontier recognized him and refused to let

him pass. "You are the wisest man in all of China," the guard said, "and if I let you pass we will lose all your great wisdom." The old man offered to write or dictate his wisdom, and the guard reluctantly agreed. The eighty-one resulting sutras or "strands of thought" became the *Book of Tao*, also known as the *Tao Teh Ching*, *Tao Te Ching*, *Tao Te King*, or *Laozi*. "Tao" (pronounced "Dow") is an uninterpretable universal absolute most frequently translated as "the way," "Te" (or "Teh"; pronounced "Tuh") is the highest virtue or character, and "Ching" (or "King") means "book."

The wisdom of old age, modesty in clothing and manner, being content with few possessions, and leading a simple life symbolize Taoist values. Mountains as a destination have, in many cultures, symbolized a higher power or higher consciousness, a place for quiet reflection or final rest. Examples include Denali (Mount McKinley), Peru's Machu Picchu, and the Himalayas.

Some scholars suggest that the sutras were probably chanted or recited from about 3000 BCE or earlier, before writing was developed. Even after the development of ideographs, the earliest Chinese writing, a "book" wasn't a single volume but a bundle of scrolls or painted bamboo sticks easily mismatched over time. That may be why the sutras are not in logical order and some are not internally consistent.

Lao Tse lived at the same time as K'ung Fu Tse, who is known in the West as Confucius. They lived in different provinces and there is no evidence they ever met. There is a legend, however, that tells of their meeting. It is said K'ung Fu Tse, learning of the great wisdom of Lao Tse, sent a messenger to invite him to visit. But at the instant the messenger disappeared at the horizon, a man rode up on a donkey. It was Lao Tse, who approached K'ung Fu Tse saying, "I understand you wanted to meet with me." This legend points up the difference between these two great philosophers. Lao Tse was more mystic and valued meaning and simplicity, knowing more about less. K'ung Fu Tse was more pragmatic and valued order and knowledge— the more detailed the better. Governments were run according to his teachings in the *Analects*, but lives were guided according to the *Tao*.

A New Translation

The following new translation begins with sutras describing Tao followed by those on Teh. It seems likely the original was arranged in a similar, but more logical, sequence, and this order seeks to return to a smoother, more logical flow. Each sutra in this translation ends with its traditional number given in parentheses. Some phrases and lines have been relocated within a single sutra for improved continuity, but nothing has been omitted and all eighty-one sutras are included.

There are some wording changes to remove age and gender bias clearly inconsistent with the Tao such as "truly wise" instead of "sage" or "wise man." Unlike other translations, this one is based on a comparative content analysis of Chinese, British, and American versions (see "References" at the end of this book). It is a revision of the author's 1962 version and reflects continued study and comparative content analysis since then.

THE TAO TEH CHING

Tao Is Absolute and Eternal

There is something mysterious, without beginning, without end, that existed before the heavens and the earth. It is silent, unchanging, and infinite. It is everywhere and it is inexhaustible. It is like a great mother of everything. I do not know its name but if I must name it I call it Tao. If I must describe it I call it supreme. Supreme means never-ending. Never-ending is far-reaching. Far-reaching means eventually returning. Tao is supreme. The universe is supreme, earth is supreme, and humanity is supreme. There are four supremes and humanity is one of them. Humanity is subject to the laws of the earth. The earth is subject to the laws of the universe. The universe is subject to the laws of Tao. Tao is subject only to the laws of its own nature. (25)

Tao Is Beyond Words

The Tao described in words is not the real Tao. Names are useful but cannot describe Tao. Tao is the unnamed ultimate source of everything. Named, it is the great mother of everyone and everything. To see it one must be without selfish motive. With selfish motive only the surface, and not what is within, is seen. Those two observers are similar because they are both human, but they differ in insight. (1)

Tao Is Everywhere

Tao is so great it can be used to infinity. It is inexhaustible. Like nature, it is in all things and has been in all things from their beginnings. With it, sharp edges are rounded, different angles intersect, various colors merge, and chaos is calmed. It is so deep its source is unknown and it is older than thoughts of God. (4)

Tao Is Super-natural

Tao is all-powerful, absolute, but it claims no title. Though it is incredibly simple and seemingly insignificant, the world has not understood it. If leaders used it everything would follow freely, according to its nature. Heaven and earth would join and there would be peace with little effort. As civilization grew there was a need to name everything. With names it is wise to know when to stop. Knowing when to stop prevents harm. Tao is like a stream that flows into rivers to the vast open sea. (32)

The Greatness of Tao

Tao is everywhere, to the left and to the right. Everything is created from it. Nothing is rejected by it. Everything exists from it, but it makes no claim to what exists. Without ulterior motive, it seems insignificant. Being the source of everything it is truly great. Because it does not claim greatness its greatness shines brightly. (34)

Like a Drawn Bow

Tao is like a drawn bow. The highest part is lowered and the lowest part is raised. Overall length is shortened and overall width is widened. Tao lowers the highest and raises the lowest, but in the world the high are raised and the low are lowered. Who can take from the high and give to the low? Followers of Tao give without taking, achieve without claiming credit, and selflessly avoid recognition. (77)

Tao in the Home

You can know about the world without leaving home. You can see Tao in nature without looking closely. You can know it without scholarly study. The truly wise do not travel far to know Tao. They see without looking, know without studying, and achieve with seemingly little effort. (*47*)

Walk the Path

Walk the path of Tao, avoiding bypaths of useless knowledge. The way of Tao is easy to follow but many prefer the bypaths. It is like palaces that are well kept, but surrounded by untilled fields and empty storehouses. Being well dressed, wearing expensive jewelry and swords, gorging oneself with food and drink, and having much money and property is excessive and invites crime. It is not the way of Tao. (*53*)

Without Tao

Without Tao, "humanity" and "justice" become official goals. When "knowledge" and "wisdom" are goals there is more hypocrisy. When "good parenting" and "obedient children" are goals there is more family discord. When "loyalty" is publicly praised there is more inefficiency and corruption. When there is such darkness and disorder there is a need for great leaders. (*18*)

Existent Nonexistence

Looked for, it cannot be seen. It is invisible. Listened for, it cannot be heard. It is inaudible. Reached for, it cannot be touched. It is intangible. Though contradictory, these three are one. The outside is not bright. The inside is not dark. It is infinite, without beginning, without end. It is formless form, existent nonexistence. It is elusive. Meet it and it has no face. Follow it and it has no back. Be one with it and you will know true reality and be warmly welcomed into Tao. (*14*)

The Value of Nonexistence
Thirty spokes join at the hub, but using a wheel depends on the place where nothing exists. Clay is shaped into a vessel, but using it depends on the inside where nothing exists. Doors and windows are set into walls, but using them depends on open spaces where nothing exists. So there is value in using what can be seen, what exists, and there is value in using what cannot be seen, what is nonexistent. (*11*)

Existence from Nonexistence
Going forward in Tao seems like going backward. Being open to it is the key to receiving it. Everything is produced from Tao yet its existence comes from nonexistence. (*40*)

The Wide Net of Tao
One who is bold and evil is destructive and will be destroyed. One who is bold but good is supportive and will be supported. Good and evil are in both kinds of boldness but Tao flows only to one. Even followers of Tao have difficulty with this. Tao is not contentious but is a subject of contention. It has no voice but its message can be heard clearly. It does not command attention so it attracts attention. It is a wide net from which nothing is lost. (*73*)

Content Contentment
If the world followed Tao thoroughbred horses would work the farms. When the world forsakes Tao cavalry horses graze in

the parks. Discontent is a great weakness. Greed is a great sin. Ruthless ambition is a great defect. Be content with contentment, with just enough, and you will find peace. (46)

Tao Seems Foolish

When the world thinks Tao is great it is great in a different way. It is in the difference that it is great. If it were like anything else it would be insignificant. There are three great treasures of Tao to cherish and preserve. The first is love, without which nothing is possible. The second is moderation, to know the mystic balance. The third is humility, to know that we come from nothing and return to nothing. Without these treasures there is darkness. Love is so strong it conquers all. There is no defense against it and Tao arms with love those it protects. (67)

Teh in Tao

Tao generates and energizes everything and Teh sustains it. Tao is all-powerful and Teh is all-sustaining. Both flow naturally in everyone and everything. Together they nurture and protect, cultivate and comfort. They are productive without being possessive. They dominate and they recede. In leaders this is hidden Teh. (51)

The Scope of Teh

What is firmly planted is not easily uprooted. What is firmly held is not easily lost. In this way generation follows generation. Be open to Tao and Teh will be there. Open families to Tao and Teh is there. Open the city to Tao and Teh flows. Open the nation to Tao and Teh grows. Open the world to Tao and Teh is worldwide. In this way Teh is a measure of one's self, family, city, state, and nation. Know this by seeing it in action. (54)

The Seen and Unseen

Teh flows from Tao. Tao flows from nature, invisible, intangible, and obscure. It is invisible but it can be perceived. It is intangible but it can be felt. It is obscure but it can be understood. In it is the basic life force. This has been true and self-evident since ancient times. Realize this by these signs and what is within you. (21)

Teh of the Ancients

Those ancient followers of Tao, so wise, subtle, and profound. They understood so deeply that they themselves were misunderstood. They were not easily recognized and so their strength was undiminished. They were as cautious as someone crossing a frozen stream in midwinter, as alert as someone traveling through a strange land, as unassuming as melting ice, as dignified as an honored guest, as receptive as a valley, and as friendly as freely mixing muddy water. Who can make sense of a world as clouded as muddy water? Like muddy water, left alone it would clear itself. Can such stillness remain? Agitate it and it becomes cloudy again. Act selflessly with Tao and there is movement without the clouding of selfish motives. Hardship can be endured as movement continues. (15)

Teh Knowing

Who knows says nothing. Who speaks does not know. Stop the senses. Do not puzzle over their questions as you undo their tangles. Be one with the light to better see the ways of the world. This is mystic unity beyond accepting or rejecting, risk or benefit, better or worse, and it is therefore a valuable treasure. (56)

More from Less

When the truly wise see Tao they seek it more. When others see Tao they are content to look no further. Those who do not see it laugh at it. If it were not laughed at it would not be Tao. Tao enlightenment can seem dull, progress like regression, and the straight path crooked. Having Teh can seem lowly like a valley or tarnished metal. Strong Teh can seem weak, sufficient Teh insufficient, and supportive Teh frail. Great space has no edges or corners. Great form can be formless. Great ability is limitless. Great music can be extraordinary. Tao is like that, formless, hidden, extraordinary, yet energizing everything. *(41)*

Words, Facts, Acts

Words of truth are not necessarily impressive. Impressive words are not necessarily true. Who has Teh has no need to argue. Who argues does not have Teh. Who has Teh does not study trivial facts. Who studies trivial facts does not have Teh. Those with Teh fulfill life for others and are therefore full of life, give freely of themselves and are therefore wealthy. Tao serves absolutely. Those with Teh serve selflessly. *(81)*

Teh Strength

It is wise to know others but wiser first to know yourself. It is strong to master others but stronger first to master yourself. The truly wise are content to have just enough and therefore they are self-sufficient. They move with just enough speed and so they are true to their own nature. They are sincere and so they endure. They are remembered and so they are immortal. *(33)*

Less Is More

Which is more important, that the world know you or that you know yourself? Which is more valuable, money or your mind? Which leads to greater evil, winning or losing? Strong attachments and great wealth risk loss. Being content with just enough prevents extremes. Know when you have enough and there is less to lose. Know when to stop and there is less danger. Knowing this is to endure. (44)

Have and Have Not

Who has Teh does not boast of it. That is a sign of really having it. Those who boast of it do not have it. Teh is selfless, never selfish. True morality is also without selfish motives. Public morality makes claims and can have selfish motives. Custom and tradition make claims and have selfish motives. Without Tao public morality becomes the rule. Without morality public well-being becomes the rule. Without public well-being conformity becomes the rule. Without conformity laws and regulations become the rule. It is a process of confusion and disorder. Followers of Tao endure because they focus on deeper truth, below the surface, what is inside. They are receptive to one and not the other. (38)

Water Motive

The highest motive is to be like water. Water is essential to life but never demands a fee or proclaims its importance. Instead, it flows humbly to the lowest level and in this way is much like Tao. In their homes the truly wise love the land, the ground on which homes are built. In their hearts they love what is natural and genuine. In their friendships they are caring and giving. In their talk they are sincere. In governing they act in good faith and with good will. In their work they are reliable and quietly efficient. Selfless serenity is their goal, a sign of Tao, and with it there is no strife. (8)

Water Power

There is nothing humbler or more yielding than water. yet it can wear down what is strong and rigid. There is nothing like it. The weak can overpower the strong. The flexible can overcome the rigid. Everyone can see this but few use it. The truly wise know that to lead a nation they must humble themselves to that nation. Who bears the sins of the world is fit to lead the world. This truth can seem illogical. (78)

The Eternal Constant

Open yourself, realize inner harmony, be one with everyone and everything. When distracted, return to nature. Returning to nature is to find inner harmony. Finding inner harmony is to realize your destiny. Realizing your destiny is to know the eternal constant. Knowing the eternal constant leads to great wisdom. Not knowing it is a great misfortune. To know it be impartial. Being impartial is to be unbiased. Being unbiased is to be balanced. Being balanced is to return to nature. Returning to nature is to be like Tao. What is like Tao endures free of harm. (16)

Sparing Talk

Nature is sparing in its talk. Unusually strong winds or heavy rains seldom last very long. Where do they originate? Within nature. If nature is so sparing in its talk how much more then should you be? Follow Tao and Tao will follow you. Follow Teh and Teh will follow you. Fail to follow them and you will fail. Follow nothing and nothing follows you. Welcome Tao and Tao will welcome you. Welcome Teh and Teh will welcome you. Ignore them and they will ignore you. Have no trust and no one will trust you. (23)

Moving On

What is still is easily held. What has not yet happened is easy to anticipate. What is rigid can be easily broken. What is small can be easily moved. Cope with problems early, before they grow. Having a still mind prevents distress. A tree with an arm's girth of trunk grows from a tiny sprout. A nine-storied terrace rises from one clump of dirt. A thousand-mile journey begins with the first step. Overdoing can undo. Overreaching can cause one to lose one's hold. The truly wise do not overdo and so do not undo anything. They do not overreach and so do not lose anything. Failure can occur close to success, so be as careful at the end as at the beginning. The truly wise value what is not valued. They do not long for what they do not have. They unlearn what has been learned. They seek what has been lost. They help everyone and everything, and they follow nature and their own nature and so never interfere with nature's way. (64)

Good in Evil

Tao is at the source of everything, treasure for the good and refuge for the bad. High-sounding words and deeds can be used for evil. Why reject them? At the crowning of leaders it is better to give the gift of Tao rather than jade and prize horses. Why did the ancients value Tao? It is because the good who seek it will find it and the evil who find it can be forgiven. So Tao is a treasure for everyone. (62)

Positive Indifference

Nature is indifferent to life. Everyone and everything is treated like a sacrificial straw dog. The truly wise are indifferent in the same way. They realize humanity is much like a straw dog and the universe is like a bellows that empties, yet fills. They proceed as they recede and produce as they are reduced. This is beyond words and it is useless to try to describe it further. (5)

Teh Security

Having Teh is like children whom poisonous insects and snakes do not bite and whom predatory animals and wild birds do not attack. Hands are weak but can grasp firmly. They are too young for sexual desire but grow in good health. They are too young to speak but freely voice their feelings. This requires inner harmony. To have inner harmony is to know the eternal. To know the eternal is to be truly wise. Disharmony upsets everything and interferes with nature. It is not the way of Tao. Whatever opposes Tao cannot last. (55)

Double Enlightenment

Good roads have no barriers. Good speakers are not misunderstood. Good planning does not need detailed notes. Good security does not rely on locks or fences. Good knots hold but are easily untied. The truly wise are good because they are good to others and no one is rejected. They help everything without reservation. This is double enlightenment. So the good are lessons to the bad. Those who are not good are lessons to the good. Those who do not value such teachers and students are misguided, even if intelligent. This is subtle wisdom. (27)

Teh Trust

The truly wise are selfless. People's needs are their needs. The good are treated with goodness. Those who are not good are also treated with goodness. This is the goodness of Tao. They trust those who trust them. They also trust those who do not trust them. This is the trust of Tao. The truly wise accept the world impartially and in good faith and people remain themselves. Like innocent children the truly wise accept everyone as members of one family. (49)

Life in Death

Life leaves when death arrives. There are thirteen parts of living and dying—four limbs and nine openings. Why? It is because living tips the balance toward dying. Those who know this are safe from the horns of the wild buffalo and the claws of the tiger. Weapons of war find no place to pierce. Why is this? It is because it is not yet time for death. (50)

Understand Misunderstanding

My message is easily understood and put into practice. The world does not understand it or put it into practice. My words have an ancient source. My actions have meaning and purpose. When this is not understood I am not understood. The few who understand are better for it, proof there is value in what I say and do. It is better to wear common clothes and carry your valuables in your heart. (70)

Similar Differences

To value only beauty is in itself a kind of ugliness. To value only good is in itself a kind of evil. Opposites share the same basic energy. Existence and nonexistence differ only in cause and effect. Easy and difficult differ only by degree. Near and far differ in distance. Low and high differ in height. Shrill and deep differ in tone. Before and after differ in time. The truly wise accept this and work despite differences or differing words. So they teach by example rather than by words. They accept everything and reject nothing. They are productive and not possessive, freely sharing what they do. They achieve without claiming credit, and their achievements are self-evident and can never be taken away. (2)

The Danger of Extremes
There is a danger in extremes. Pull a bowstring too far and you wish that you had let go before. Hone a sword blade too well and it wears too soon. Fill your house with jade and gold and you invite thieves. Be arrogant and proud and you hasten your own failure. Reach your goal and be satisfied to go no further. This is the way of Tao. (9)

The Risk of Extremes
Whoever stands on tiptoe is unsteady. Whoever walks with long strides cannot long keep up the pace. Those who make a show of themselves cannot really shine. Those who seek glory cannot become the best leaders. The self-righteous lose the respect of the people. The self-centered lose the love of the people. In Tao these are excessive and inappropriate. Even in worldly matters they should be avoided and the followers of Tao avoid them. (24)

Why Avoid Extremes?
Who tries to win the world will lose it. The world is sacred and beyond reach. Trying to seize it interferes with nature. Accord-

ing to the Tao some things proceed and others recede. Some things move quickly, others slowly. Some succeed by strength, others by weakness. Some are active, others passive. The truly wise avoid extremes, excess, and exaggeration. (29)

Yin-Yang

To have mystic Yang but also mystic Yin is like being a stream that flows through the world. Being like that stream is to have constant Teh like the innocence of a child. Having the light of Yang but also the shade of Yin achieves a high standard. Having that high standard is Teh connecting with Tao. To achieve yet be humble is like a fountain to the world that reaches high, yet flows to the lowest level. Being like that fountain is to have mystic unity. Divide mystic unity and its parts become tools. In the hands of the truly wise those tools are a means to an end, never an end in themselves. They are all part of Tao. (28)

Unity Is Balance

In Tao there is unity, oneness. Oneness is the source of duality. Duality is the source of triples. Triples are the source of everything. The shade of mystic Yin is on the back of everything. The light of mystic Yang is on the front of everything. Balance comes from their interaction—which is equal, like breaths taken in and breaths let out. Being alone and unwanted is feared, but even the best leaders experience these feelings. Losing can be beneficial and winning can be harmful. I say what many have said before, a major teaching: the violent come to violent ends. (42)

Motiveless Yin

Tao never acts directly, yet it is indirectly in everything. If leaders did the same, everything would improve naturally. If leaders did the same, selfish motives would become selfless simplicity. With selfless simplicity there is no need to compete. Without competition there is harmony and all is well in the world. (37)

Mystic Mother Yin

Yin is the mystic mother and she is everywhere. She is at the source of heaven and earth. Thinly veiled and delicately formed, find her and let her help you. She is infinite and inexhaustible. (6)

Virtue in Being a Fool

Stop amassing trivial knowledge and you will be less encumbered. What is the difference between agreement and disagreement, beauty and ugliness, fear or being feared? Such nonsense never ends. Others seem happy as if at a feast or celebration. I alone seem as aloof as a newborn baby too young to smile or a wandering person without a home. Others seem to have more than they need. I alone seem to have less. Others are bright and knowledgeable. I alone seem dull and uninformed. Others see things clearly. I alone seem to be in the dark. Others are clever and quick-minded. I alone seem as unsettled as the vast ocean and aimless as a soft breeze. Others choose a set path. I choose a different way, sustained by a mystic mother. (20)

Mystic Virtue

Can you keep mind and spirit on the path of Tao? Can you breathe softly and gently like a newborn baby? Can you purify yourself to perfection? Can you love and lead without self-interest? Can you be the receptive mystic Yin beginning to ending without weakening? Find your way while knowing nothing? Be productive and supportive of others without being possessive? Give freely of yourself without obligating others? Help without getting in the way? This is a mystic virtue. (10)

Quiet Strength
That which decreases first increases. That which weakens is first strengthened. That which is rejected is first accepted. That which is taken must first be given. This is subtle wisdom. The flexible overcomes the inflexible. Being gentle overcomes strength. Strength is best kept hidden, like fish that swim under water. (36)

Soft-Hard Strength
What is soft can penetrate what is hard. What is nonexistent can permeate the existent. There is advantage in working quietly and taking no action. Few things are as useful as silence and working quietly. Few know this lesson without words. (43)

Inner-External Needs
Colors can flood the eye, sound can deafen the ear, and taste can overpower the tongue. Anxiety and ambition can unbalance the mind. Selfish striving can interfere with a good life. The truly wise satisfy inner needs and avoid selfishly satisfying external needs. They accept one and avoid the other. (12)

Serene Balance
If a great achievement seems a failure, this does not lessen its value. What is full can seem empty, but this does not lessen its

usefulness. What is straight can seem crooked. Great skill can seem awkward. The most eloquent can seem boring. Moving soothes being cold. Resting soothes being overheated. Sharing and peace soothe a troubled world. *(45)*

Flex!

Newborn infants are soft and yielding. The dead are hard and unyielding. Living plants are soft and pliant. Dead, they are withered and brittle. Being hard, unyielding, withered, or brittle is like death. Being yielding, soft, or pliant is like being fully alive. So a headstrong army will lose just as an unyielding tree snaps from the axe. The place of the rigid is below. The place of the flexible is above. *(76)*

Yield to Be Strong

Bend and you will not break. Yield and you remain whole. Empty yourself and you will be filled. Grow up and you will not grow old. Have little and you will have enough. Have too much and you will be needy. Therefore, the truly wise seek and hold mystic unity close. They are good examples to all. They do not seek recognition, so they are worthy of recognition. They do not boast, so they are worthy of praise. They earn trust by trusting others. They are able leaders because they do not seek to control. They win because they do not compete. The old saying is true: "Bend and you will not break, yield and you will remain whole." *(22)*

Learn Less and Less

The world's way of knowledge is to learn more and more every day. The way of Tao is to learn less and less every day. Seeking trivial knowledge lessens inner peace. Find and master the indirect way and all will go well. The world belongs to those who know how to let go of it. Try to control it and it is already beyond reach. (48)

Fortune, Misfortune

Both good fortune and misfortune can cause problems. High and low feelings can coexist. How? Good fortune raises and misfortune lowers. There is anxiety with both. Be selfless and there is no anxiety. Those who try to better the world are worthy of leading the world. Those who love people are worthy of being loved by people. (13)

Know That You Do Not Know

It is best to know that you do not know. Not to know that you do not know is sick. The truly wise are not sick because they see it as such. They are sick of sickness. So they know what they know without being sick. (71)

The Rope of Tao

Do not boast of your wisdom. Avoid trivial knowledge. Everyone will benefit. Stop proclaiming humanity and justice and there will be more caring and responsibility. Stop extravagance and abundance and there will be less crime. These three avoidances are strands braided into the strong rope of Tao. It is strongest when tied to a pure mind, simplicity, selflessness, and restraint. (19)

Selfless Power

Heaven and earth endure because they do not exist for themselves alone. The truly wise are like that. They choose to be last and so they are worthy of being first. They empty themselves and so they are fulfilled. They are selfless and so they fully realize their true selves. (7)

Mother-Child Serenity

The world's beginning can be seen as a mother giving birth. Know the mother and you can know her children. Know her children and you can remain close to their mother. Live this way and there will be no fear of life or death. Eyes and mouth closed, life has few problems. Eyes and mouth open, life has more problems. Accept weakness to overcome weakness. Use inner light to increase enlightenment. This is the way of Tao. (52)

Heavy-Light Strength

Heaviness can overpower lightness. Serenity can overpower restlessness. The truly wise travel lightly but keep their heavy baggage close by. Though there are many sights to see elsewhere they are happy to stay home. Should a leader of ten thousand chariots be heavy or light? Regard everything lightly and you may lose sight of deeper truths. Be deeply troubled and you may lose yourself. (26)

Yin-Yang Leadership

The world will follow without fear, serene and secure, a leader who holds close the great Yin-Yang. Passing strangers stop for music and tasty food but not for the words of Tao that seem unappealing and meaningless. Look for it and you cannot see it. Listen for it and you cannot hear it. Use it and it is inexhaustible. (35)

The Best Leaders

The best leaders are inconspicuous. The next best are respected, the next are feared, and the next are defied. If you do not trust people, people will not trust you. The truly wise are humble and soft-spoken. When the best leader's work is done and goals are achieved, the people say: "Look what we did together." (17)

Lowly-High Leadership

Why do rivers and seas overflow lowlands? It is because they lower themselves. And so to be elevated by people, lower yourself to them. To lead, walk behind. The truly wise are above but no one feels their weight. They lead but no one feels blocked. They do not quarrel so no one quarrels with them. They are not aggressive, so no one is aggressive toward them. The world would respect and never tire of such leaders. (66)

Lead Humbly

Eternal mystic unity makes the heavens constant, the earth stable, and the valleys fertile. It uplifts the human spirit. It brings everything into existence. It brings success to the best leaders. Without it the heavens would not be constant, the earth would be unstable and the valleys infertile. Without it the human spirit would falter. Without it the best leaders would fail. What is high depends on what is low, just as a chariot depends on its many parts, moving or still. So, the best leaders humbly depend on everyone and everything. It is better to be as coarse and plain as a stone than to be like polished fine jade. (39)

Normal, Abnormal

Lead indirectly and quietly and people are happy. Lead aggressively and loudly and people are unhappy. Happy and unhappy are opposites. Why? What is normal? Normal can become abnormal. What looks good can become evil. It is confusing. The truly wise are square but without sharp corners, they can wedge in or out without sharp angles, pointed but not painful, and they are bright without blinding. (58)

Lead with Moderation

Moderation is important to lead well. Moderation is to yield and in yielding there is strength. With that strength anything is possible. When anything is possible there are no limits. Without limits power also has no limit. This is the mother principle. Be one with it and your leadership will continue and endure firmly rooted in Tao. (59)

Harmless Leadership

Lead as you would cook a small fish. Be careful not to overdo it. Leading with the strength of Tao weakens evil. Evil may continue but do less harm. When evil is less harmful leadership is also less harmful. Then neither leaders nor the people are harmful or harmed and everyone benefits. (60)

Prevent Evil Excess

Do not encourage competition and there will be less rivalry and malice. Do not encourage wealth and there will be less theft. Do not encourage abundance and there will be less harmful excess. Truly wise leaders encourage emptying to be fulfilled and weakening craving to strengthen character. When many people are without cunning and selfishness those who are cunning and selfish do no harm. Lead with restraint and all will be well. (3)

Move Graciously

When people lose respect for leaders it is time for change. Do not crowd them and there will be more room in which to move. Do not reject them and they will not reject you. Therefore, be yourself but use restraint. Accept yourself without undue pride. Cultivate what is inside and not just what is outside. (72)

Simplicity

Ancient followers of Tao did not use it to enlighten others but to increase simplicity and decrease useless trivia. Leadership is difficult when people value useless trivia. Lead with useless trivia and you are the people's enemy. Lead without useless trivia and you are the people's blessing. Understand this and you understand mystic Teh. It is far-reaching and it returns with greater strength and harmony. (65)

Achieve Indirectly

Achieve indirectly, with quiet efficiency. Savor the tasteless. Raise the lowly. Consider the few as many. Respond kindly to unkindness. Resolve what is difficult while it is easy, the complex while it is simple. The world's major problems can be solved while they are minor. The hardest work can be done with less effort. The truly wise do not actively seek greatness, so greatness comes easily to them. A promise lightly made is difficult to keep. Consider everything easy and everything can become difficult. The truly wise know what can be difficult and therefore have fewer difficulties. (63)

Teh Healing

There is seldom complete healing after severe injury. Settling a heated dispute leaves some hatred behind. How can this be prevented? Those with Teh defend the weak and do not seek vengeance. Those without Teh attack the weak and seek vengeance. Those with Teh do their duty. Those without Teh let others do their duty. There is equality in Tao. Goodness freely flows through it for the good of all. (79)

Why People Suffer

People suffer when taxes are high. That is why they suffer. People resist leaders who are oppressive. That is why they resist. People do not fear death when leaders value life and do not interfere in the people's lives. That is why people do not fear death. Those who do not interfere with life gain more from life. (75)

Small Is Great

An ideal organization or state is small, with few people. It has tools and machinery but little need for them, weapons but no need to brandish them. It has vehicles but no need to travel far. The people so love it there that they do not leave. They are satisfied with knotted ropes for counting, simple food and clothing, modest homes, and simple customs. Other organizations and states are wary of one another. Though distracted as if by barking dogs and crowing cocks, the truly wise are content being where they are, as they are. (80)

Greater Is Lesser

A great nation is like land where streams descend. It is a meeting place of mystic Yin, quiet, unpretentious. With gracious receptivity it subdues mystic Yang. A great nation lowers itself to a smaller nation and thus merits its support. The smaller nation lowers itself to the greater nation and thus merits its support. So, whatever is low is worthy of support from others. Greater and lower nations need such people. When both kinds of nations have met their needs the greater nation should still be supportive. (61)

The Secrets of Selflessness
Skilled leaders are not aggressive. Skilled warriors do not lose self-control. A winning strategy is to never antagonize the enemy. The best way to lead others is to share equally with them and adapt to them. This is the secret of selflessness. It is to be one with ancient Tao. (68)

Be Lawful, Not Full of Laws
Lead by doing what is right. Wage war by clever strategy. Control the world by letting go of it. How do I know this? Too many rules weaken the people. Too many weapons invite trouble. Too many crafty people mean more wrongdoing. Too many strict laws mean more offenses. Therefore, the truly wise simplify and people understand more. They are serene and people are content. They are selfless and people's lives are enriched. Being unselfish encourages a simplicity like that of uncarved wood. (57)

War Is Not Tao
Weapons of war invite war. Followers of Tao avoid using them. Teh leadership favors peace. Leaders without Teh favor war. When war cannot be avoided weapons are used only as necessary. The best policy is restraint because there is no joy in war. To find joy in it is to delight in violence. Peace brings happiness. War brings sadness. Who delights in violence is not fit to lead. Military commanders in war officiate at many funer-

als. When many are killed the grief for both sides should be shared, even in victory. (*31*)

When War Is Inevitable

Followers of Tao counsel leaders against the use of force. Force can backfire. Thorn bushes grow when armies are on the march and bad times follow. The need to protect should never be for selfish reasons. Achieve victory then stop, without pride or boasting, without flaunting superiority or indulging in the spoils. Instead, regret not preventing war because it is not good to conquer by force. Overdoing invites decline. It is not the way of Tao. What departs from the way of Tao cannot endure. (*30*)

Secret Weapon

Military strategists would rather defend than attack and retreat a foot rather than advance an inch. Doing so is like marching in place, not really going anywhere. It is to seem unprepared but actually ready. This is winning passively and it is a secret weapon. There is no error more tragic error than underestimating the enemy. Doing so risks losing everything. When evenly matched armies battle, the passive side is more likely to win. (*69*)

Capital Punishment Warning

When people do not fear death, why threaten them with it? When people fear death, they are threatened by it. Who then wants to be executioner? There is only one supreme executioner. Assuming that role is like giving unskilled workers the axe of a master carpenter. They could chop off their own hand. (*74*)

Last Words?

We have no record of any last words of Lao Tse but Sutra 67 may well be what he would have said:

> I leave you with three jewels. Guard them and keep them safe. The first jewel is love, to know that living is giving, that everyone is your brother or sister, and that the one great law of life is love. Without love nothing is possible. The second jewel is moderation, to know the mystic balance, avoid extremes, and accept differences as a way to grow. The third jewel is humility, to know that you are born with nothing and will die with nothing, but also to know that to die and be remembered is to have immortality. (67; *edited*)

5 Transitions: The *I Ching*

With only the I Ching *a corpse could lead the world.*
Ancient Chinese saying

THE BOOK OF CHANGES (*I CHING*)

The *I Ching* may be the world's oldest human relations manual. Evidence of its great importance in ancient China is the saying: "With only the *I Ching* a corpse could lead the world." Confucius (K'ung Fu Tse, ca. 551–479 BCE) called it "the perfect book." That its advice makes sense today, five thousand years after it was first chanted and, at some later point, written, proves its value and validity. How much of what is written today will survive the next five thousand years? This version was prepared by a comparative analysis of Chinese, British, and American translations from CE 1859 and a study of underlying Chinese philosophy.

According to legend, Emperor Fu Hsi (ca. 2800 BCE) was fascinated by the markings on the back of a tortoise. He saw there eight basic designs of solid lines and dashes. *Ch'ien* (father force, or heaven) is three solid lines and means creation and Yang; *K'un* (mother force, or earth) is three lines of two dashes each and means receptivity and Yin; *Chen* (first son, or storm) is two lines of dashes above and one solid line below and means activity, movement, or disturbance; *Sun* (first daughter, natural wood, or still air) is two solid lines and one line of dashes and means gentle passivity; *K'an* (second son, or the sea) is one line of dashes, one solid line, then another line of dashes and means change or flexibility; *Li* (second daughter, or warming fire) is one solid line, one line of dashes, then another solid line and means dependence, clinging, or coexisting anger and frustration; *K'en* (third son, or mountain) is two solid lines and one line of dashes and means stability, balance, or repose; and *Tui* (third daughter, or lake) is one line of dashes and two solid lines and means happiness and joy.

Fu Hsi observed how the pairs of symbols were complementary: *Ch'ien* and *K'un* (heaven and earth); *K'en* and *K'an* (mountain and sea); *Chen* and *Sun* (storm and still air); and *Tui* and *Li* (water and fire). He compiled sixty-four different hexagrams and believed that these were the basis of life and behavior. He is also credited with developing writing, so *I Ching* may be one of the first books written in China.

In ancient China the text of each hexagram was written calligraphically on a yarrow stick. While concentrating on a question or personal problem, the sixty-four sticks were held in one hand and loosely shaken. The stick that protruded furthest or that fell from the bundle was considered the answer to the question or advice on the matter of concern. The hexagrams can be used in the same way by preparing sixty-four slips of paper, each marked with a numeral from one through sixty-four.

The papers should be folded three times, placed in a container, and shaken to mix them thoroughly. Finally the person seeking advice must, with eyes closed and while concentrating on the question or problem, remove one slip.

A variation is to use sixty-four cards, each marked with a numeral from one through sixty-four or with an image of a hexagram glued or printed on it. The cards are shuffled, and the person seeking advice must, with eyes closed and while concentrating, draw a card at random. Or the cards can be shuffled and then placed facedown and the top card drawn. Another method is to toss two coins six times, while concentrating. Each throw should be noted as a single line for two heads or two tails, a broken line for one head and one tail. The corresponding hexagram is then read. This takes more time. Others find it useful to simply read one hexagram a day for personal guidance.

The ancient Chinese sometimes used *I Ching* in small groups. The people faced north and prostrated themselves three times. They then formed a close circle, sitting with legs crossed (though not necessarily in the lotus position). The *I Ching* was then passed around the circle three times clockwise through rising incense smoke. This was done in silence with everyone concentrating on the question or problem for which guidance was sought.

In ancient times *I Ching* was placed as high in a room as possible and wrapped in fine silk. This was believed to preserve its purity and power. *I Ching* was considered sacred, used only for personal guidance or serious discussion. Please respect this ancient belief.

THE 64 *I CHING* HEXAGRAMS

▤ *1. Be Dragon Strong (Ch'ien)*

Take time to further develop your inner strength. Avoid taking direct action. Be observant and think carefully. Calmly reflect and contemplate to bolster your self-confidence. Consult with those who are wiser and more knowledgeable. Avoid extremes. It is a time to quietly cultivate and develop the four attitudes of firmness, strength, moderation, and justice. Do this in silence and solitude.

▤ *2. Serve Lovingly (K'un)*

Be more perceptive. This avoids problems before they develop. Let abilities and skills flow naturally. With quiet efficiency do, but don't overdo. Apply just enough effort. In time of stress take firm control of yourself and you will protect yourself from it. Lead indirectly by following or appearing to follow. Your good work identifies you to others, so make it a labor of love. Success flows naturally from loving service, devotion to duty, and quiet efficiency.

▤ *3. Grow and Go (Chun)*

Grow and move on at a comfortable pace, checking who and where you are along the way. Observe situations closely, carefully, seeing everything, missing nothing, and you will easily see the source of any trouble. If action is needed, use firm but appropriate action. Accept help from others but do not become dependent on them. Do, but don't overdo. Be sure of yourself and what you are doing, and move ahead cautiously.

䷃ 4. Learn Well (Meng)

Life from birth to death exerts a continuing pressure. Protect your individuality or the stresses of living may change you into someone else. Along the way, accept and graciously share with those lesser than you. Develop values based on inner strength and use them with self-restraint and good judgment. Be more yourself and emulate others less. Be gracious and modest. Doing otherwise is foolish and will be embarrassing. To learn well, realize that you must experience some discomfort.

䷄ 5. Wait (Hsu)

Stop, look around, and listen carefully before taking action. Do one thing at a time or you will fail. If a problem is complicated, realize that it cannot be solved quickly or simply. Indecision will only make it more difficult to solve. Accept reality and be firm in your convictions, but not unreasonable or antagonistic. Confusion is not continual, so pause from work to relax. Take time to keep the goal clearly in sight. Realize that no situation is hopeless. Be receptive to the help of others, accept it with sincere gratitude, and your situation will improve.

䷅ 6. Conflict Is Opportunity (Sung)

Do not take the initiative alone. Join with others. Withdraw gracefully in an impossible situation. Live according to your means. Work diligently to assure your future. Do not envy others. If you are in error, being steadfast won't bring success. Contemplate nature to find inner peace and contentment. Be moderate, feel the balance, and you will do the right thing. More problems mean more opportunities to grow. Feelings of satisfaction come from finding good solutions. Lasting happiness comes from problems solved.

䷆ 7. Lead (Shih)

If your cause is just you will succeed. Find and use the right channels. Respect those in authority, despite any personal differences, as if they earned and deserved their leadership roles. The best leader shares in the good and the bad with everyone. There can be no success without effective leadership. Discord and dissent lead to failure. When facing odds against you, save your strength by gracefully withdrawing. Strong leadership is needed when facing what seems certain failure. Share recognition and rewards freely and wisely according to contributions, abilities, and needs, but be careful not to place power in the wrong hands.

䷇ 8. Unify Yourself (Pi)

Be as real and natural as uncarved wood. Be who you really are and preserve your integrity, dignity, and honor. Overdo, and you lose some of your real self. Be disloyal, and you lose honor. It is wise to accept those who come to you for help. Do not force yourself on others. Do not deceive. Do not criticize unjustly. Know that to achieve unity requires mutual trust and respect. Without these qualities there can be no unity and no success.

䷈ 9. Be Moderate (Hsiao ch'u)

Move ahead but as difficulties come slow down, and become less forceful and more thoughtful. Using moderation prevents strain that can wear you down and limit your effectiveness. Rushing blindly ahead causes stress that drains energy. Be flexible and maneuver deftly with the situation. Explore alternatives and weigh the consequences. Share with your friends and be supportive because together you will find greater strength. Success comes by degrees and peaks and does not last.

☰ *10. Be Tactful (Lu)*

Accept your position, however humble, and be content. Hold simplicity and freedom in regard. Be tactful and moderate or you will fail. Regardless of how unreachable they seem, goals can be achieved with tact and moderation. Without tact and moderation there is uncertainty and greater risk of failure. Look back over your life and you will see that success followed when these tactics were used.

☷ *11. Grow Personally (T'ai)*

Be a friend, especially as you succeed in life. Achieve with moderation. Realize your individuality. Be realistic in all situations. Explore alternatives and new opportunities. Consider only reasonable risks. Experience changes you, but know that there can be no growth or progress without change. Change helps you to be aware of your personal development. Be friendly to everyone at all levels. Being aggressive may be effective but that need passes quickly and can cause trouble. Accept the inevitable and try as best you can to remain calm in any situation. Regardless of how bad a situation looks, there is always some good in it.

☰ *12. Cope (P'i)*

Working for the unworthy can be difficult. In such a situation it is wise to withdraw to preserve your dignity and integrity. Your friends will understand. Respect unworthy superiors for their positions, rather than for their personal qualities. Use your best judgment when possible, and not theirs. You might succeed by following them but you will feel used and ashamed. Do your best where you are. Do not overstep your authority. Think of alternatives. Be prepared for whatever happens. Know that no situation continues indefinitely. Even success and happiness have their limits.

☲ *13. Be a Friend (T'ung jen)*

Though you are a friend to everyone some will not respond to you as friends. There is a limit to friendship and it can cause problems for you. Where there is distrust there is distance. Where there is distance there can be deceit. Stand by your convictions but remain friendly. Others will see that you mean well and will accept you and your opinions. In time, friendship develops, problems are overcome, and relationships deepen, but still keep in mind that friendship has its limits. Be happy. Progress is possible and it is positive and good.

☲ *14. Achieve Real Wealth (Tayu)*

Real wealth is based on both external and inner factors. Real external wealth is in knowing the dangers of possessions and governing yourself accordingly. Real inner wealth is in knowing the dangers of being possessive and governing yourself accordingly. Your thoughts and those of your friends help you to continue being truly wealthy. Doing good with your money and possessions also helps. Do not use friends, money, or possessions for yourself alone. Subdue your cravings, be kind, sincere, and humble. Do otherwise and people will react negatively to you. You will then be alone, with only your money and possessions, and no longer truly wealthy.

☶ *15. Be Humble (Ch'ien)*

Be humble and you will meet with less resistance. Humility is a virtue and should be continually developed. With it you are able to appreciate recognition and honors but remain the same person as before. With it you can follow superiors and appreciate those who work with and for you. When successful you can be considerate even to those who oppose you. When unsuccessful you can be considerate to yourself and not become bitter. You can then lead by example in good and bad situations.

☷ 16. Be Happy (Yu)

Relax and be happy. Be serene but aware of the slightest change and ready for active or passive response. Be aware of natural tendencies to depend too much on others, indulge in excessive pleasure, or seek too much power and money. Enjoying an occasional treat is reasonable and adds to joy and happiness, but should never be done to excess. To be happy, be sincere and accepting. Help others to be happy in the same way. This helps everyone. Satisfaction comes from coping with and solving the problems of everyday life. This brings strength and motivates you and others to greater achievements.

☱ 17. Interact (Sui)

Remain true to yourself though your goals may change. Associate with those who disagree with you as well as those who agree. Associate with those less experienced as well as those who are more knowledgeable. Meet with better people to help you avoid the superficial and artificial. Deceitful people will approach you and you may tend to depend on them for the rewards they can provide. Rise above this. Preserve your integrity. Let excellence be your goal. Integrity and excellence are positive qualities that bring success and are enduring.

☶ 18. Be Insightful, Not Inciteful (Ku)

Solve problems while they are simple. Be aware that there are consequences to any change. Be aware that it takes time to build strength. As you respect your parents, also respect authority, even when you disagree with it. Act with deliberate speed, but not so quickly as to cause confusion. Do not allow ignorance to continue. You can achieve and be recognized for good work, sometimes with the help of others. Remaining a safe distance from the world helps increase self-awareness and self-improvement. Do these things and you can make something of yourself of enduring value.

☷☱ 19. Make Progress (Lin)

Succeed by doing what is right, even though others disagree with you. Those who do not clearly see what is right will follow one who does. When you have power, use it wisely. Reflect and be perceptive, or trouble will follow. Success comes by doing what is right, having right thoughts, and sharing with others who do the same. To lead, find those who are able, delegate some of your power to them and give them freedom to use it. Be receptive and helpful to all who come to you. Doing these things helps everyone.

☴☷ 20. Be Aware (Kuan)

Stop and check your perception. You may not be fully aware of what's happening. For others, this may not be very important, but it is important for you. Success depends on your close attention to the situation and finding an effective way to manage it. Success comes from using correct perception and good judgment. When you succeed, help others to do so as well, especially when you are in a new position. This helps you as well. Be realistic and take a good look at yourself, not as a lone person but as one interacting with others. Knowing how, where, and when to fit into society and in life is a worthy goal.

☷ *21. Appreciate Consequences (Shih ho)*

When you are punished, realize the justice in it. Serious offenses receive greater punishment. You may feel humiliated, even though you were guilty. This is understandable. Life is complicated. Everyone makes mistakes. Resolve to do better and grow from the experience. If you were not punished would you have learned anything? If you were the judge would you have been as fair? React negatively, and evil grows inside you out of proportion and with feelings of shame or guilt.

☶ *22. Be Yourself (Pi)*

Resist the urge to appear to be what you are not. Be yourself. Resist the urge to enjoy possessions for their own sake. Enjoy life instead. Resist the tendency to rest on previous successes, to take yourself and others for granted. Instead, continue growing. Choose personal over material growth. There are limits to material growth but no limits to personal growth. When enlightened you are a friend to everyone and everything. When enlightened you know the truth of yourself, others, and the world.

☶ *23. Cope with Deceit (Po)*

Beware of deceit. It undermines organizations, damages character, and spreads negative feelings. Be honest and sincere to those who are deceitful but do not use their methods. It may seem that they succeed and that there is no way to stop them. Stopping them requires courage, perseverance, commitment to higher values, and help from able, trusted people. It is not easy but it is not hopeless. Deceit weakens in the light of truth and good. Evil has within it the seeds of its own destruction. Remain on the side of truth and right and you cannot be destroyed.

䷗ 24. Minor Setbacks (Fu)

Obstacles and setbacks need not be losses. Use them to regain your balance, then continue to move on. You will recover more easily with good self-control. Trying to be like someone you admire can help. You may tend to do what is practical rather than what is right. You may use a quick solution rather than what is best for the long-term. That is not good for you even though no great harm is done. Collaborating with strangers can be helpful but it is better to collaborate with friends because friends help you to be yourself. Be aware of your weaknesses. Don't make excuses. Take care. Move ahead hurriedly, and you risk great loss.

䷘ 25. Keep It Simple (Wu wang)

Childlike simplicity is a virtue that should continue to be developed and used. It is doing what is right because it is right. Material wealth comes in time. There will be minor variations. The real you can be strong and resilient, so be yourself and you will do no harm. When misfortune comes, let it come. Let nature take its course. Problems can then resolve themselves without the need for any action. Accept reality, whatever it may be, and you will be part of the nature that brought it to you. Oppose it, and you will be alone.

䷙ 26. Control Yourself (Ta ch'u)

Maintain self-control when facing serious problems. Even if a situation seems desperate, do not act in desperation. Calmly center yourself in your inner strength. Help can come from others who faced a similar problem. Be aware that danger remains even after the problem seems to have faded away, and remain alert. If confronted with great force, meet it quickly and with unique tactics. If you understand the source of a problem, you can better control and solve it. Use these methods to overcome difficulties and move ahead.

☰ 27. Help Yourself and Others (Ii)

There are tendencies to be selfish, and to envy, abuse, or use others. Nothing good comes of this. There is always a need for able people who know their strengths and weaknesses. Try to be like someone you admire. Follow that person's example or advice. You cannot always succeed alone. Share what you know with others. Doing these things empowers you and you can succeed against the odds and help others to do so as well.

☰ 28. Know, Then Move Wisely (Ta kuo)

Careful study of important issues has strengthening force. Insight can come from others, even those below you, so guard against overconfidence. Moving too quickly, unwisely, or against good advice can cause more problems and worsen the situation. Do not trust only those above you, ignoring others, or you will sink deeper into trouble. Use your inner strength and that of others. Do what is right. Trouble may seem to continue but doing the right thing is reward enough, keeps you on track, and helps you improve yourself.

☰ 29. Have Hope (K'an)

Situations seem hopeless when one does the wrong thing or feels lost. Continue either way and problems worsen. Try too hard and problems multiply. Problems cannot be solved instantly, but only by degrees and with ingenious solutions. Take no action until it is the right time or the solution presents itself. Do otherwise and problems can become more complicated. Proceed honestly, sincerely, and at the right speed. Proceed without flattery, intrigue, or gift-giving. If ambition drives you too hard there will be more trouble. Apply just enough force to overcome obstacles. Do but don't overdo. Use your strengths or your weaknesses will overpower them and you will fail.

☲ 30. Avoid Confusion (Li)

Too many details confuse a situation. The solution is easier when you make a reasonable search for the major cause or the seed idea. Growing old can mean being overwhelmed by the many details of everyday living. Overwhelming details can lead to believing that life is dark. Growing old can give the impression that life is vain. Seeing life as vain can lead to cynicism. Look inside yourself to see if you have these unhealthy beliefs. If so, how much have they grown? Do not be misled by them. Return to your core and restore your values, the heart of your being. Do not be misled by the details of a situation but go to its center, the heart of the matter.

☱ 31. Use Influence Wisely (Hsien)

Influence is a powerful force and it is not always easily seen. You influence others without being aware that you are doing so. Your influence is weak when you are overly submissive, sentimental, ingratiating, or distracted. Your influence is also weak when you lack self-confidence and when your words are unconvincing.

☳ 32. Value Maturity (Heng)

Only the mature endure. Being impulsive or using excessive or careless force is not mature. Be yourself and control yourself, or trouble will confront you from all sides. Your good intentions will not then be of any help and neither will custom or tradition. Being mature means having good judgment, doing the right thing at the right time. This is difficult for those in high office because their duties can cloud their vision, drain energy, and increase anxiety.

☰☶ 33. *Withdraw Serenely (Tun)*

There is a time when it is best to withdraw, when there is no better choice. In such a situation, withdraw quietly and gracefully. If there are experts nearby use them to help your withdrawal and not interfere with it. Accept the reality of the situation and proceed without further weakening your strength and self-image. Do not allow the situation to weaken your convictions. Lesser people are unable to do that. Timing is important so move carefully and in good time. Be ready for whatever happens. All this requires careful thought and planning. The need to withdraw should be obvious, as if it speaks by itself.

☰☳ 34. *Be Patient (Ta chuang)*

Despite your best efforts your position is discouraging. You have more enthusiasm than needed, so be careful not to overdo it or you will fail. Opportunity will come, so use your enthusiasm to help develop your strengths to be ready. Using too much energy now will be destructive, so feel for the balance. Be patient, act with moderation, and all will be well. Be keenly aware of the situation. Do not be indifferent or your energy will fade. Do not be overly aggressive or the situation will worsen.

☲☷ 35. *Succeed in Failure (Chin)*

Remain calm if you do not succeed or are passed over for promotion. After being promoted it may seem to you it is more difficult to communicate with superiors. Do the right thing and you will succeed and be rewarded. Move on. You will not be alone. Be deceitful and you will be treated deceitfully. Succeed with self-awareness and self-control. Do not look back at failure and disappointment. Correct wrongdoing with special care when it involves those you don't know.

☷☲ 36. Overcome Misunderstanding (Ming ii)

Though you earnestly try to do the right thing, you will sometimes be misunderstood, criticized, or ridiculed. Nevertheless, remain true to yourself. It hurts, but it is not deadly. Persevere, and you will grow stronger. Success comes in time. When it does, be moderate, and problems will be more easily solved. When you are deeply immersed in a problem, withdraw to conserve your power and preserve your values. This requires courage and insight. Be aware that when everything seems dark you may not clearly see your duty or the sources of help around you.

☴☲ 37. Stabilize the Family (Chia jen)

A stable home and family requires balance. Being permissive is unbalanced. Children are more likely to have problems later. Being strict or permissive should be in balance but tilted a bit toward being more strict than permissive. A wife who accomplishes her tasks with care does so for the good of the family. Government should do the same for the good of the people. A wife who manages money well does so for the good of the family. Government should do the same for the good of the people. A husband who is firm but moderate and fair ensures peace and unity in the family. Government should do the same for peace and unity throughout the nation.

☶ *38. Overcome Confusion (K'uei)*

Mistakes increase under pressure or in conflict. Do not seek those who leave you in a time of need. They will return by themselves. Do not seek to remove those who make trouble in a time of need. They will leave by themselves. Differences and distrust separate people. Fellowship and trust bring people together. In desperate situations it is important to be true to yourself and your values. Make friends in the enemy camp. You will achieve your goal and friendships will grow. Do these things and all will be well.

☶ *39. Overcome Obstacles (Chien)*

A great obstacle is in your path. It is wise to take action at just the right time. The best solution is the one best suited to your skills and values. Sometimes it is better to refrain from action and remain strong. Sometimes it is better to take action with others and be stronger together. Sometimes it is better to take action alone and attract allies to your side. Sometimes it is better to do nothing and defend rather than attack. Choose which is best.

☶ *40. Stop, Then Grow (Chieh)*

When there are no obstacles it is time to stop and do nothing. Strengthen your position by patiently eliminating bad influences. Do it with moderation. It is best now to make new friends. Do not let reward or victory spoil you. Renew yourself. Stay on course. Doing these things assures future success. You will gain insight and strength and be better able to overcome any obstacle. Some will disagree with you but they will see that you are trying to do the right thing.

☲ 41. Be Selfless (Sun)

Offer your support to superiors if no harm comes from it. Be loyal if you can do so with dignity and honesty and without harm to you. Two can be close because of similar interests but not three, because their differences will be too great. Rid yourself of bad habits and you will enjoy richer friendships. There will be fewer obstacles to success. Anxiety will be lessened. Power and influence will be great and growing and can be used to good effect. Others will see that you are sincere and well-meaning, and will join with you.

☲ 42. Use Higher Power (Ii)

Help comes from a higher power, so use it wisely. You will succeed if your goodness harmonizes with that of the higher power. Learn from failures but do not dwell on them. If you are asked to settle differences, be just and moderate and you will earn trust. Do what is right because it is right. Free yourself of any selfish motive. If you misunderstand the situation, or act too quickly, you will fail and others will no longer trust or confide in you.

☱ 43. Hold On (Kuai)

Act in haste without careful thought and planning and mistakes will follow. Be attentive and perceptive and no mistakes will follow. It is time to be friendly but firm and not antagonistic. You may at first be misunderstood. Resist being provoked or you will risk losing control. You must be true to your convictions to overcome major obstacles. Success is near but cannot be achieved alone. The problem you now face will return again.

☰ 44. *Neutralize Negatives (Kou)*

When under the influence of a negative person, cope with it with moderation, without acting too forcefully. You may be tempted to join the other side. To make such a major decision requires much insight, but wait, and the situation will be resolved without the need to decide. You are not in the majority, so your support is limited. Be gracious and accepting to those below you. Criticize and you will be criticized. If you do not speak truth, your reputation will be damaged.

☷ 45. *Unify (Ts'ui)*

Share in a spirit of unity with others. Ask for help and you will receive it. You will then think more clearly and feel more satisfied. The spirit that draws you and others together is beyond your knowledge. Be open to it, do not resist it, and success follows. If anyone is in your way, seek and befriend another who can help. Any embarrassment passes. Friends trust and work closely together toward the common goal. You will be accepted, gain a leadership role, and be successful without much effort. You will be misunderstood and some will use you. Do what is right and these problems will fade. The person you befriend will misjudge you and you will feel sad but the unifying spirit will carry you through.

☷ 46. *Onward, Upward (Sheng)*

The way is open to you. Your sincerity, ability, and dedication are evident and well received. Since there are no major obstacles, you may want to be more forceful. Realize that your success is in part spiritual and from above—from caring friends and superiors who believe in you. Keep this in mind, to prevent taking your success for granted or believing that you have achieved it on your own. Proceed thoughtfully and carefully or nothing will go well.

䷁ 47. Enlighten Yourself (K'un)

If you are not aware and attentive you will suffer. Unseen problems, even simple everyday situations, will confuse you. It may even seem negative when some things go well. Help will come from someone in authority who seeks your advice. Find and center yourself with quiet contemplation. Confusion makes you more sensitive and more apt to make mistakes. Graciously helping those below you will also help you. Even problems at levels above and below you can be overcome in this way. Control yourself. Don't let difficulties get you down. You will continue to improve as you reflect on mistakes and use the lessons they provide to overcome weaknesses.

䷯ 48. Overcome Darkness (Ching)

If you find yourself alone amid negative forces, this may be because you have been ignoring your better nature, and not making full use of your abilities. Your superiors may not have used your strengths. Your friends will be sad to see this. You may suffer this way for a time until you stop, reflect, and regain control of yourself. It will be a worthwhile effort. Realize that when the nature and abilities of solidly grounded leaders flow naturally, they succeed and are able to do good. As they are admired and respected, they help and inspire others.

䷰ 49. Achieve Success (Ko)

When you are frustrated, do not strike back. Act when the time is right and only after careful planning and support from others. Though you may not be aggressive, some may still see your actions as excessive. They will later understand that this was not so. Success comes from strict values, inner strength, and moderation. When people see these qualities in you they will accept and follow you. As major goals are achieved, move on to minor goals. This completes the cycle of success.

☷ 50. Restrain Yourself (Ting)

Negative influences weaken as you continue along your path. Continue, though others may envy you. Sometimes problems seem larger than your ability to solve them. Sometimes your strict values do not seem useful at a lower practical level. Great effort can be wasted on problems that you are unable to solve at the time. Great needs can go unmet when you lack the resources to satisfy them. In such situations all is for naught and can end in humiliation. There is wisdom within you but you must want to find it and use it wisely. If you remain receptive and humble you can connect to the higher power that is the source of all goodness.

☳ 51. Overcome Anxiety (Chen)

Unforeseen events increase anxiety, but not for long. Failure can be costly, but there are other ways to succeed. What is lost can be regained. Repeated failures cause continued stress. These can be overcome by solving problems with just enough force. Know there will always be problems and they are best solved by finding their causes. Without moderation problems multiply. Avoid this cycle of anxiety. You will be criticized for it, but doing the right thing will save you from much needless pain.

☶ 52. Stop, Look, Listen (Ken)

Stop and study yourself and the situation. Concentrate, contemplate, and do not be distracted. Your superiors may do wrong, but you are not responsible for it. You are responsible only for what you do. Use times of inactivity to reflect on deeper thoughts that lie beyond the everyday routine. Be yourself and do the best you can as you seek deep inner peace. Use words wisely and sparingly. If there is nothing to say, say nothing and avoid embarrassment. Doing these things connects you to the nature of the universe.

☴ 53. Keep Going (Chien)

If you are unskilled, you learn slowly and may be ridiculed. That kind of learning is long and painful. As skill increases so also will self-confidence, and social and material rewards will follow. Overdo, and problems increase. This becomes serious until you realize and adjust to your strengths and weaknesses with humility and openness. Though deceitful people are in your way, you will succeed, achieve your goals, and be a model for others.

☳ 54. Move On Slowly (Kuei mei)

When superiors trust you, return their trust by working with quiet efficiency. Weaknesses in the group will be overcome by your skills and good faith. Realize that it is better at this time to succeed by doing good indirectly, gently, from within, rather than failing by working directly and forcefully. Do not compromise your values or let ambition cloud your vision. Do not act falsely, to impress others, but genuinely. Doing these things will increase your enlightenment.

☳ 55. Find Your Way (Feng)

You will gain by joining with a future leader. Others attempt to use the leader and get in your way. Take no action or you will be resented by them and distrusted by the leader. As others get attention your influence will fade. Be honest and sincere with the leader. Do the best you can. Your influence will increase and your position will improve. Your ability and loyalty will win a promotion. Guard against success spoiling you and distancing you from family and friends.

☰ 56. Be Real (Lu)

When you are impatient you are impulsive, too eager to get ahead at any cost. This is not good and will bring trouble. It is better to be humble and value your integrity. When impatience drives you on you will succeed but become more selfish and un-caring, and lose what you have gained. The unworthy have high ambition but low ability. They are unhappy because they are strangers to themselves. If you are like that you will succeed for a time, with help from influential people, but you will become more selfish, uncaring, and not worthy of success.

☰ 57. Care Carefully (Sun)

Control yourself when confused or influenced by negative forces that you do not understand or that you are not aware of. Find them and be aware of them, and they will weaken. Fail to find them or to be aware of them, and they will grow stron-ger. Success is limited when you find many negative forces and there is no time or way to cope with them. Success depends on increasing strength, self-respect, and the respect and trust of others. Continue on that path by checking before, during, and after each step.

☱ 58. *Seek Light, Not Heat (Tui)*

Even as you experience inner peace, you may continue to crave pleasure and be tempted to store up possessions. Protect your dignity and integrity. Misfortune will result if you pursue immediate pleasure without regard for the consequences. Distress grows from indecision about when and how to pursue pleasure. It is better to pursue the higher pleasure of enlightenment. It is often selfishness and foolish pride that give rise to craving for material things. Beware of people too who will try to use you for their own selfish pleasure.

☴ 59. *Be Natural (Huan)*

Misunderstanding is not likely when needs are satisfied naturally. To abuse anyone or anything alienates others from you. To accept anyone or anything attracts others to you. Proceed with moderation and there will be no regrets later. To have love, give it away. To find someone, lose yourself. To know this is to be enlightened, selfless, not self-centered. In troubled times this is the key to well-being and peace. Danger is reduced and there can be safety and security.

☵ 60. *Move Wisely (Chieh)*

Know your limitations and do not go beyond them. It is time for action. Wait and it will be too late. Plan carefully, then set the plan in motion and all will be well. Do otherwise, and fail. Do not waste time or effort. Understand all aspects of a problem. Take just enough action at just the right time. Earn respect by following the same rules that you impose on others. Overdo it, and you invite resistance. Realize that even when justice is swift and fair, some evil can persist.

䷼ 61. Open Up (Chung fu)

It's time to think clearly, openly, aware of and ready for possible problems. There will be bad results if your mind is closed. There will be good results if your mind is open. Rely too much on others, and you will feel inferior and insecure. These feelings do not reflect the real you. Remain calm and receptive, and help will come from above. When that happens, absorb and use it, because it is for you alone. As you apply it, choose words carefully, because it may be difficult to put what you have received into words. Be natural, sincere, true to yourself, and you will be one with the Mystic Unity.

䷽ 62. Be Moderate (Hsiao kuo)

Don't hurry. Be calm, patient, and ready to use good judgment. You will succeed but you need help from others. Act with moderation and with great care. Ignore this advice, and you will fail. If there is no one to help, wait. Be patient. A skilled helper will come and you will then succeed. Pay too much attention to details, and you will make trouble for yourself and others.

䷾ 63. Success Fails (Chi chi)

Finish work before you are confused by it. Even though you do well, those above you may not have confidence in you. Competent leaders ensure continued success. Incompetent leaders cannot continue their limited successes. Being proud and competitive in victory leads opponents to find new battlegrounds. When all is well after a victory, many problems are overlooked. Despite the facts of what happened, people are influenced by their feelings, for good or evil. Be aware of these things and avoid the risk of failure hidden in them.

䷿ 64. Plan Well, Do Well (Wei chi)

Continue to make progress despite confusion. If your timing is off you will fail. Control yourself. Maintain your strength and skill. Act when the time is right but know that you cannot succeed alone. Try to do so and you will fail. The situation now is greater than your strength and skill. How you resolve it will influence your future. Great problems require great solutions. Consider your immediate needs first. Be positive and sincere and you will get help from others. Success now will solve the problem and ensure a brighter future. Afterward, relax and enjoy the victory, but be careful to do so in moderation. Overdo it, and you may lose all that was gained.

6 Yoga: Light from India

*There are eight limbs
to the yoga tree and
its fruit is tranquility.*
Ancient saying

HINDU GODS AND GODDESSES

Hinduism is the major religion of India and may be the world's oldest religion. Brahma is its Supreme Self, the creator-god. He also appears in other forms such as Atman and Paramatman. His consort is Saraswati, the goddess of knowledge. Within Brahma there is the Trimurti, or trinity, of Brahman the Creator, Vishnu the Preserver and Cosmic Mind, and Shiva the Destroyer and Cosmic Lord. Krishna, quite similar to Christ, is the eighth avatar, or form, of Vishnu. Shiva has a dual identity: Kali or Durga, the goddess of death and destruction, and Parvati or Uma, the goddess of birth, life, and motherhood. Freud's concept of libido, the basic life force, and its two branches—*eros* and *thanatos*, of creation and destruction respectively—are clearly represented in these Hindu concepts.

There are both masculine and feminine aspects within the Hindu trinity, and these are considered "two wings of the same bird," to quote an old Hindu saying. The *Bhagavad-Gita* reads: "I am the father of the universe. I am the mother of the universe. I am the creator-of-all" (9.17). For Brahma the feminine aspect is in Saraswati, goddess of knowledge. Lakshmi is Vishnu's consort and the goddess of love.

There are lesser gods, such as Indra of the heavens, seen in thunder, lightning, rain, and snow; Agni in fire; Surya in the sun; and Yama in far and unknown countries. Hindus worship many gods and goddesses, some as gods especially revered within a particular village or family. Hindus do not find the notion of multiple deities confusing or inconsistent. It is said that Brahma's many forms are like the water present in streams, rivers, lakes, and oceans, dew, fog, rain, snow, and ice—all aspects of one thing.

HINDU LITERATURE

The *Vedas* are Hindu sacred scriptures. According to legend they are more than five thousand years old and were chanted before there was a written language. They are poems, prayers, rituals, hymns, and chants and include the mystic-philosophical *Upanishads*.

Hindu literature is extensive. The *Bhagavad-Gita* is a dialog between the god Krishna and the warrior Arjuna. *Puranas* are legends of Hindu heroes and heroines, gods and goddesses and contains the Hindu version of creation. *Ramayana* is the story of good Prince Rama and the demon Ravana. *Manu Smriti* describes and justifies the caste system, which is now illegal in India although much social bias continues to exist.

The *Mahabharata* is a collection of stories of good and evil. There are six major branches of Hindu philosophy: one emphasizing logic and reason (*Nyaya*); another focused on looking to nature for guidance (*Vaisheska*); another centered on creation themes (*Sankhya*); one consisting of physical and meditative exercises (*Yoga*); another consisting of rituals (*Purva-mimansa*); and one that contains the *Bhagavad-Gita, Upanishads,* and *Brahma Sutra (Vedanta)*. Certain Hindu gods were believed to take animal forms. This explains such customs as reverence for "the sacred cow" and the special care taken to observe these customs.

THE ORIGINS OF YOGA

Yoga probably originated before writing, but yogic literature began in about 200 BCE with the *Yoga Sutra* attributed to Patanjali. Yoga is a philosophy and system of meditative self-development. The word is derived from the Sanskrit *yuga*, which means "to yoke" or "to be one with" cosmic consciousness and Brahma. It is a structured system of self-discipline and exercises that help lead one to liberation to karmic rebirth at a higher level of existence (*moksha*) and liberation from materialistic worldliness (*moksha sastra*).

Yoga has eight "limbs," or levels, and one old Hindu saying describes it this way: "There are eight limbs to the yoga tree and its fruit is tranquility." A man practicing it is a *yogi*, a woman a *yogini*. Belief in a personal god is not necessary; an atheist can be a *yogi* or *yogini*. Yoga does not conflict with most religions. Westerners use it mainly for physical exercise and meditation.

Those thought to be closer to final liberation are affectionately referred to as "old souls." Gandhi is revered in this way.

YOGIC TRADITIONS

There are various yogic traditions:

- *Asparsha* is "no-touch yoga," and involves living the life of a hermit in the wilderness.

- *Bhakti* is ritualistic and devotional, stressing self-control (*yama*) and a selfless love of God or Nature that overcomes insecurity or uncertainty.

- *Gyana* is "the yoga of knowledge," removing ignorance by reasoning and developing "analytic will."

- *Hatha*, popular in the West, emphasizes body control through physical and mental exercises for health and well-being;

- *Jnana* is more philosophical, emphasizing meditation on reality and nonreality, renouncing what in the West is considered "real" but in yogic philosophy is "unreal."

- *Karma* is "the way of work and service," overcoming ego and selfishness by a labor of love, without hope of personal or material gain.

- *Kundalini* is "serpent power," psychic energy coiled at the base of the spinal cord, which with meditation rises up through body centers, or *chakra*.

- *Mantra* is based on chanting meditation using mantras such as "Om" or "Krishna" and other mantras selected for individual needs.

- *Raja*, or royal, yoga seeks to steady the mind by intensive self-analysis from a blend of bhakti, karma, kundalini, mantra, and jnana yoga.

Hatha yoga is popular in the West and is used mainly for

physical exercise and stress relief. Breathing and physical exercises, hand signs (*mudras*), chants, sense control, concentration (self-control), and meditation (spiritual control) facilitate progress through the eight limbs, or stages, of yoga.

A word of caution! Strictly orthodox, traditional yoga was a very rigorous discipline, probably too much so for Western taste. For example, sex was traditionally avoided because it is believed that sperm and ova prevent spiritual progress. One ancient practice of cleansing the body involved squatting over a basin of water, aspirating it up the anus. In another exercise, the practitioner swallowed a strip of surgical gauze several feet long (while holding onto one end), and then pulled it back out, which was believed to cleanse the stomach. Breathing by alternating between the left and right nostrils was thought to cleanse each side of the brain despite the fact that there is but one airway into the throat. Ancient philosophies have reflected the knowledge of the time and so were sometimes based on error, myth, or superstition; today these practices are observed only occasionally by enthusiasts.

The ancients believed that the human spirit is capable of superhuman feats (*siddhi*) and can even change nature. Experimentally verified demonstrations of such a unique ability are cases in which yoga practitioners have entered a state similar to suspended animation and have survived stays in airtight sealed chambers that would otherwise have been fatal. Used regularly and appropriately, yoga can be a tonic for the mind and body. Those who practice yoga report less stress and improved ability to cope with stress. Behavioral, medical, and mental health professions use biofeedback, hypnosis, massage, and physical exercises to induce a more relaxed state of mind, examples of how modern science perhaps unknowingly refines ancient practices.

THE EIGHT LIMBS OF YOGA

According to the yogic system, everyone has *prakriti* and *purusha*. *Prakriti* is the physical body and mind (psychophysical self). *Purusha* is pure consciousness, or meditative, spiritual awareness; it is the soul (spiritual self), independent of mind and body, that continues after death. More orthodox yoga requires the personal guidance of a guru (teacher or mentor). The first four limbs help to control external factors, or simple sensing of the world and everyday realities, while the remaining four are for more intensive self-study and greater meditative awareness. The eight limbs are sequential, to be mastered in order, though they are interdependent. Mastering one enhances mastery of the others.

1. *Yama*

Yama is self-control, self-discipline, or direct, conscious control of moral judgment. To master it requires honesty, humility, and a firm commitment to doing no harm to any living thing. Achieving *yama* involves mastering the five abstinences: nonviolence (*ahimsa*), not intentionally causing pain to yourself or others; truth (*satya*), thinking, speaking, and acting only to do good; honesty (*asteya*), never taking anything—tangible or intangible—through thought, word, or deed, that does not belong to you; purity (*brachmacharya*), abstaining from impurity in thought or behavior, even by boast or jest, or look or talk; contentment (*aparigraha*), being satisfied with what you have—preferably little or nothing—and declining purely materialistic rewards.

EXERCISE: Imagine that you are your own best friend—someone who can tell you the truth about yourself, about your strengths and your weaknesses alike. The philosopher Jean-Jacques Rousseau, the therapist Carl Rogers, and Zen Buddhists have all said that down deep inside people know the answers to the questions that trouble them, and know what is right for them. Other names for this hidden wisdom include "wisdom of the body," "the still, small voice," "common sense." Religion and therapy can help you "see yourself as others see you," but you must do the work, or "walk the walk." To experience *yama*, consciously say or do something good—something completely unexpected and unselfish—at least once a day.

2. Niyama

Niyama involves finding positive spiritual values through conscientious self-study and through making conscious, self-disciplined choices to put these values into practice in everyday life. It differs from *yama* in its focus on spiritual values, rather than on personal habits or traits. The goals of *niyama* are an open, sincere search for what is good, followed by efforts to do good. It involves being careful and caring to do no harm. *Niyama* practices include: cleanliness of the body and mind; using faults as challenges to be overcome and striving for spiritual growth instead of personal status or material gain.

EXERCISE: The "five observances" help achieve *niyama*. These are: purity (*saucha*), both outward (clean body, mind, and home) and inward (commitment to goodness and doing good); optimism (*santosha*), remaining positive regardless of any difficulties; self-control (*tapa*) through diet or fasting, meaningful speech, and earnest study; self-improvement (*svadhyaya*) through reflection, thinking, chants, and meditation; and *spirituality* (*ishvara pranidhana*), offering word and action as spiritual outreach to the cosmic, universal consciousness or Eternal Spirit.

3. Asana

Asana is appropriate position and posture control. This stage helps block distractions that would interfere with the development of higher consciousness. It ensures the proper breathing, blood circulation, and muscle relaxation that are necessary for the next five steps. Yoga positions activate internal centers of force for the maximum receptivity of higher cosmic forces. According to legend, Shiva assumed 100,000 yoga positions eighty-four times, to create humans! There are eighty-four standard yoga positions, but less than thirty-three are widely used today.

EXERCISE: Good asana involves sitting upright with legs crossed, and with each hand palm up on the leg closest to it. The full lotus position is not an absolute requirement. The object is an attentive position conducive to concentration but not so comfortable as to induce sleep or bring discomfort. Asana means "appropriate." Clothing should be loose and comfortable. Shoes should be removed. Bodily needs should be satisfied beforehand. A quiet place without distractions or interruptions is recommended. Yogis and yoginis meditate for "one watch," of about three hours, but this is not practical for most people. Twenty to thirty minutes a day on a regular schedule and with a set sequence of exercises can be effective.

Easy Position (Sukhasana). In the Bhagavad-Gita Krishna described this position as "sitting motionless, mind controlled, body and head erect, vision inward." It is a partial lotus. Sit erect on the floor with both legs stretched straight out. Use a thin cushion if you wish. Bend the right leg and tuck it under your left thigh.

Bend the left leg and tuck it under your right thigh. Pull your feet, by the toes, in toward you. The knees should be kept close to the floor, but without straining. Sit up straight, with your head erect, your eyes closed, and your hands on your knees with the palms up, fingers relaxed, and thumbs gently touching your index fingers. Be aware of your breathing and relax. If your eyes move, stare at an imaginary fixed point ahead.

Corpse Pose (Savasana). This position is especially helpful through the first four yoga stages. Many use this as the last position in a sequence that they perform daily. To assume this position lie flat on your back with your arms out, palms up, fingers relaxed, hands about twelve inches from your waist, legs straight, and feet about twelve inches apart. Be aware of breathing regularly, in an unhurried way, in and out. Use the regularity of your breathing to further relax your body. Be aware of one part of your body, then another, working from the inside outward to your arms and legs to fingertips and toes. Take your time. Repeat if needed. Relaxation should flow easily. Good signs are the head moving slowly to one side as the neck muscles relax, the jaw falling open slightly as facial muscles relax, and the feet turning slightly outward as the leg muscles relax.

Back Stretch (Pashimatasana). In a sitting position, stretch your legs out together in front of you. Lean forward, so that your head touches your knees, and your elbows touch the floor. Hold for three minutes.

The Plow (Halasana). Start from the corpse position, but with your legs together and your arms at your sides with the palms down. Raise both your legs about twelve inches off the ground and hold for a slow count of five seconds. Slowly lower them back down, count to five again, and raise them again for another slow count of five. Raise your legs higher as you become more proficient.

The Cobra (Bhujangasana). Do this three times. Lie facedown with your legs together, toes outward, and arms bent, with your hands on the floor at chest level. Lift your head and slowly raise your chest, pushing against the floor with your hands, with your legs still stretched out straight along the floor behind you. Arch your head back, so that you resemble a cobra about to strike. You may feel your spinal vertebrae lift, one at a time. Breathe evenly throughout this exercise.

The Bow (Dhanurasana). Do this three times. Lie facedown with your legs together, toes outward, and arms at your side, palms up. Raise your feet by bending your knees until you can reach and hold the right foot with your right hand and the left foot with your left hand. Pull on your feet to bring them as close to your ears as possible. This is like drawing a bow, hence the name for this position.

4. Pranayama

Pranayama is breath control to ensure body and organ stability for the "steady mind" needed to continue climbing the yoga limbs. *Prana* is the vital force in both air and breath. As fish find water invigorating, humans find *prana* in air the same. According to yoga philosophy pranic energy can be shared or given to others, though doing so weakens the giver. Gasping in a cold shower or when surprised or in pain is the body's way of taking in pranic energy. Mouth-to-mouth resuscitation, in yoga terms, is far more than providing oxygen to a person in need; there is also a spiritual element.

Some kind of breathing exercise should be a standard part of your yoga routine. Two traditional times for it were before sunrise (after completing the toilet) and two hours after sunset. An occasional deep breath helps lower the blood pressure, strengthens the diaphragm, and provides a richer oxygen supply to the lungs. According to yogic philosophy, deep breathing also releases the *kundalini* force from its center, the *muladhara chakra* at the base of the spine. Traditionally, the Vishnu *mudra*—thumb against one nostril, and the ring or third finger against the other—was used to alternate breathing from one nostril to the other because it was believed that each nostril energized that side of the body.

The Bellows (Bhastrika). This is believed to release *kundalini* force to penetrate the brain chakra (*sahasrara-chakra*). Inhale normally, hold both nostrils closed, then exhale only from the right nostril. Quickly inhale from that nostril, continuing to hold the left nostril closed. Exhale only from the left nostril, then inhale quickly through it, keeping the right nostril closed. Do this ten times.

The Bee (Bhramari). In your preferred meditation position, eyes closed, take in a deep breath, and then, while exhaling slowly, make a humming sound. The sound is called *nada* and it is believed to resonate through the body as a mantra that helps deepen meditation.

5. Pratyahara

Pratyahara is "turning inward" to control the senses by intentionally withdrawing from everyday sights, sounds, smells, and feelings of the external world. It is deliberate selective inattention, consciously tolerating but avoiding sensory stimulation to quiet the mind. The noticeable effect of this is less "mental noise" from the sensory barrage of everyday life. Chanting, singing, and mantras (a word or repeated saying) can be used to overcome the interference of everyday noise.

Traditionally gurus would choose a mantra for someone to be used only by that person and never shared with another. Mantras can be used in silence, just meditating on them, or aloud. *Om* is the "sacred syllable," an ancient mantra still widely used. It consists of three sounds, beginning with AH, the awakening and reality, proceeding through OO, the journey or astral plane, then MM deeply resonating through the body, the unifying principle. Printed mantras are used for meditation by first looking at them, then seeing them with eyes closed, imagining hearing them in a variety of voices, or actually chanting them aloud.

EXERCISE: Quiet the mind and body at what would ordinarily be hurried times, such as when you are in a crowd, running late, at a boring meeting, or in heavy traffic. You can experience *pratyahara* by ignoring an itch, an ache, or sensory signal (such as sound, smell, touch, or light). Try it by delaying answering the phone one ring longer than usual or not opening the daily mail until an hour later. Use annoying sights and sounds—like falling raindrops, a ticking clock, music you don't like, or noisy machinery—positively.

Use your ingenuity. Innovate. In your preferred meditation position, screen the thoughts that flow into your mind. Sift them, gently turning them aside as a gardener turns the soil with a trowel. Use this image of the gardener to help turn aside any intrusive thoughts so that you can meditate more effectively. Another useful image is ocean waves that wash slowly across a beach, one after another; in the same way, intrusive thoughts may come and go, but they do not interfere with nature. Mastering *pratyahara* helps develop a calm reflective mind and an attitude of cheerful optimism.

6. Dharana

Dharana is intense, undistracted, finely focused attention often referred to as "steady mind" or "one-pointed concentration." It follows naturally from the fifth limb (*pratyahara*) that enables you to minimize and eliminate distractions, whatever they may be. *Dharana* is used to naturally settle into deeper concentration using an object, thought, feeling, or idea to the degree that you are so into it that you "become one with it" or "experience oneness with it." Achieving this stage requires practice and experience in neutralizing and clearing the mind of everything else.

EXERCISE: Fix your attention on a flower, tree, or shrub, a design in a carpet, draperies, or clothing, a part of a picture or scene, a part or function of the body, a single instrument, tone, or rhythm in music, or the sound of an appliance or engine. A lighted candle in a darkened room has been widely used for *dharana* meditation. The flame consists of contrasting light and dark areas, from bright white and yellow in the outer area, to orange, and then to blue deep inside. The wax ranges from solid to semisolid to liquid, and from opaque to clear. These qualities make it an ideal meditative subject. A glass of water is another good subject. It is solid but wet; the glass reflects light differently from its sides; and the water is peaceful, serene. Likewise, a sharpened wood pencil has the smoothness of its enameled sides, the velvet of the smooth wood, the solid, black lead, and the pliable rubber eraser in its hard, cold brass collar. Or try a peach kernel, an apricot or olive pit, a rubber band, a newspaper.

7. Dhyana

Dhyana differs qualitatively from *dharana*. *Dharana* is more a state of fixed, deep concentration and *dhyana* is an eager, open, receptive state of meditative awareness. It moves the mind and spirit from the external meditative objects or images of *dharana* to a deeper, internal, more spiritual meditative level. It feels different. *Dharana* is more like working at a craft, more attentive to process and detail. *Dhyana* is unhurried, tranquil, restful reflection without motive. *Dhyana* mind is in its freest aspect "open as the sky."

EXERCISE: Daydreaming, reverie, drifting into a peaceful sleep, savoring your favorite food or favorite music with eyes closed, resting comfortably. *Dhyana* is "poetic drifting" or "artistic repose." Zen Buddhists call it "falling off an imaginary log." Others call it "falling down your own well" or "on the down escalator." You can develop *dhyana* by looking at the sky on a clear night, the moon and stars against the black sky. An ocean beach has been a meditative subject for centuries — the sand and surf, textures of sand and tree bark, seashells and stones, the sea breeze, sun glittering on waves far out at sea, clouds. Sunrise and sunset, mountain ranges, forests, desert or your own immediate surroundings offer opportunities for meditation.

8. Samadhi

In *samadhi* the mind is connected to cosmic or universal consciousness (*kaivalya*), the highest level of yogic meditation. It has achieved *moksha,* or the level of meditative awareness from which you can never fall. The last three limbs were like a journey from inner to outer space. *Dharana* was learning the practical skill and the self-control of piloting the ship of self on its meditative course. *Dhyana* was piloting from inner toward outer space despite any and all obstacles.

Samadhi is arrival in the new world of the universe at large, a cosmic consciousness. The ship of self then moves with the force and freedom of the universe, not affected by anything human, earthly, or material. It is being yoked to the universe, cradled in its arms. This eighth and final step is a very personal achievement, one that no one can ever take from you, a truly mystic experience.

Samadhi can "flash" through any of the other yogic steps at any time. Ironically, we are surrounded by it, but not many are able to see it. We are immersed in all the raw material with all the subject matter needed, but it is a solitary journey that we must begin, continue, and complete ourselves. The *Mundaka Upanishad* describes this process:

> Take the secret teaching as the bow,
> Place on it the arrow sharp from meditation,
> Draw it with a mind full of at-oneness,
> Thus, arrow, target, and mind are eternal.
> Let OM be the bow and self be the arrow,
> Let at-oneness be the target;
> The target is struck through awareness,
> Thus arrow, target, and mind are one.

Signs of *samadhi* are realizing *mystic unity* ("all is one"). At-oneness (*savitarka*) is the beginning of *samadhi.* When you can be at-one with whatever is, without names or the need to name, you enter the *samadhi* state. Then there is no knower and no known—no I, you, it. One is all, all is one, there is no one, and all is all.

Samadhi brings a fresh breeze to mind and body, joy, deep peace, and clear, pure thinking and reasoning. The total effect is to realize ultimate reality, the absolute, a cosmic consciousness. Patanjali, the Father of Yoga, described *samadhi* as arising in seven stages:

1. Deep, sincere longing for truth (*subhecha*)
2. Proper inquiry (*vicharana*)
3. Fading of ego, intellect, and previous learning and conditioning; development of intuition, insight, enlightenment (*tamanasa*)
4. Purification of the body through yogic exercises and the mind through meditation (*satvapatti*)
5. A serene, tranquil state of mind beyond worldly matters and problems (*asamsakthi*)
6. A state in which the external world no longer has dominion, in which it has become unreal and impermanent (*pararthabhavina*)
7. Ability to see the Absolute, the Eternal, Universal Consciousness in everything (*turya*)

EXERCISE: Slowly read, and then meditate, on the following two ancient messages. The first is from the *Svetasvatara* of the *Bhagavad-Gita* (Mukerji translation, 1929):

> The One God has many mystic aspects: creator and created, consumer and consumed, builder and destroyer beyond building and destroying, in darkness and light and sustains all these opposites. In creation there is darkness and light, either, both, and neither. As a child cannot escape the mortal mother so the universe cannot escape the Immortal Creator.

God cannot be understood except by God-think-
ing and God-mood, hidden and unhidden, like one
seed from which all flowers bloom.

The second is from the *Rig Veda* (Ingbert-Gruttner translation, X:129):

Who knows for certain? Who can say so?
How did creation occur? How was the universe
born?
Gods came after this world's formation.
Who then can know the true origin?
No one knows.
He who sees it from the heavens,
He surely knows—or perhaps he does not.

Potential Problems

To achieve *samadhi*, three *guna* (Sanskrit, meaning "tendency")
must be transcended:

- *Sattwa*, difficult to translate but meaning pure essence, the
  "what" of "it" (whatever is contemplated). In the West this
  is a focus on fine details, the goal of the sciences and a deductive process. In the East the approach is inductive and
  intuitive, a search for meaning rather than for "hard facts."
  Socrates defined intelligence as "to know that you don't
  know," knowing something well enough to know its limits.
  Einstein said, "There are no certainties."

- *Raja* is the active principle; it is powerful, passionate,
  aggressive, proclaiming its importance. You experience it
  when it is as if what you are reading jumps off the page or
  when you are deeply moved by something you have seen or
  heard.

- *Tama* is the inertia that must be overcome to develop yogic
  skill. It is seen in laziness, indifference, apathy, and being

"stuck" or "blocked." It is anything fixed, unmoving or immovable, static, or constant.

Learning to drive a car requires factual knowledge of the controls and principles of operation. That's *sattwa*. Actually driving develops skill based on experience. That's *raja*. Tamas is having to push yourself to learn, take the time, maintain interest and motivation, and use self-control to apply the energy needed. Sunrise, sunset, clouds, and flowers are *sattwa*. The bright radiating sun, moving clouds, and blossoming flowers are rajas. It's *tama* when you fail to notice them. To reach *samadhi*, you must reach beyond the three *guna* and transcend them. *Guna* are useful at earlier stages of meditation, by experiencing them then choosing to move on past them.

Three states of mind, or *avastha*, can block yoga mastery:

- "Dispersed mind" (*kshipta*) is a mind pulled apart by the three *guna*, confused and indecisive.
- "Stupid mind" (*mudha*) is when *sattwa* and rajas are weak, and tamas strong, and the person hears but does not listen, or listens but does not learn.
- "Unstable mind" (*vikshipta*) is in a person who has *sattwa* and rajas but no tamas, and is therefore unstable.

Other obstacles are a "tossing mind" (*vikshepa sakthi*), a "blocked, biased, or resistant mind" (*avarana sakhti*), and a "self-centered, selfish, materialistic mind" (*mala*). Like any body- or character-building system, yoga can fail if it is not done enough or not done well. "Cramming" yoga, trying to do everything at once or too hurriedly, can be as ineffective as superficial study or limited, sporadic practice.

Nonconformists who use yoga as part of a counter-culture limit its usefulness. The object is self-mastery, and not social protest. Yoga should not be used as an escape or an obsession to avoid personal responsibilities.

SIDDHI

Siddhi are yogic feats above and beyond what is normal for most people. They have been reported in yoga literature for centuries. There are eight classical siddhi: divine power (*ishit-va*), the power to create things; overcoming gravity (*laghima*) to become weightless and travel at great speed; astral projection (*prapti*), allowing one to move anywhere instantaneously; invisibility (*prakamya*), allowing one to make oneself invisible to others; control (*vashitva*) over living beings and objects; super-consciousness (*mahima*), seeing everything in the universe first-hand; microconsciousness (*anima*), making oneself as small as an atom; and magnification, the power to increase gravity, such as one's weight, so as to become immovable.

None of these classic siddhi have been scientifically authenticated. Some may have been hypnotic phenomena experienced in deep trance from intensive meditation or induced by a revered guru. Exceptional physical and mental achievements from yogic practice *have* been authenticated. Despite a short lifespan for others in their culture, yogis and yoginis often reach much older ages. They also show a calmer, more tranquil adjustment to conflict and stress, greater insight and intuition, and a mastery of the senses. Some have had foreknowledge of their own death and have serenely accepted it. Paranormal and extrasensory perception have been reported, such as telepathy and clairvoyance. While not as dramatic as the eight classic siddhi, they are beyond normal behavior for most people who are not practitioners of yoga.

Yogic Meditation

Here are some suggestions to help make yogic meditation more effective:

Time

The minimum time for effective meditation is twenty minutes twice a week, or every other day. Beginners should meditate daily until a good level is achieved. Usually this takes a month. Many practitioners recommend meditating before meals because this slows digestion. Mornings or late afternoon are better than night, because while meditation is relaxing it does *not* help you sleep.

Place

The ideal is to have a special place for meditation. This can be a comfortable chair (a recliner or overstuffed chair is best), sofa, bed, or carpeted floor with a cushion. Many people just lie in bed. Avoid uncomfortable places and positions. You can have your own small "temple" or "ashram," located in a corner of the room, where you can place a candle, small flower vase, and a picture (such as a still life, landscape, or seascape) or small figure of Buddha, Asklepios, Jesus, Athena, Isis, Osiris, or another deity. An ashtray or incense burner is optional; some people are allergic or find incense irritating. A man's handkerchief makes a nice "altar cover." This scene itself can be used for meditation and visualized in meditation when you are away from it. For meditation, turn out or dim the lights. Many meditators use a candle. No interruptions!

Position and Posture

Sitting (or lying) down is a good meditative position. Sit on a bed, with your back against the wall or against the back of the bed, with your legs extended straight out. Or sit upright in a soft, comfortable chair, in a recliner, or on a cushion on the floor. Cross your legs and place your hands on your thighs, palms up, with hands touching at the knuckles or with one hand atop the other. Don't intertwine your fingers. You want minimal contact between body parts. Interlaced fingers can feel swollen.

You do *not* have to get into the lotus position! The object is to minimize distractions, from the room or from your own body. It's best to remove shoes and loosen any tight clothing. You can meditate while lying in bed, although beds are for sleeping and it is best if you can use another place. The yoga "corpse pose" involves lying on your back on a carpeted floor, with your head on a pillow, legs parted, feet about twelve inches apart, arms extended at your sides, hands about nine inches from your body, palms up, and fingers relaxed. This position is simple, easily done, and free of most external objects and contact with your arms and legs. This offers the opportunity to experience a free-floating feeling, which is conducive to a higher level of meditative awareness.

Candles

The candle is a classic, centuries-old object for meditation. Place the candle in a holder or small dish. Light it. Concentrate on the flame, which is multidimensional. The outside is brightest— white and yellow. Inside there is a blue oval, and a small open area of no flame. The wick glows orange-red at the tip, black beneath that, and white where it enters the candle. The candle itself is of hard wax, soft to the touch. Where it burns it is clear like water. It slowly pours, semisolid, down the candle's side. What is the message of the candle, of its parts? What are its lessons? Are you a candle? What would being a candle teach you?

Mantras

A mantra is a specially selected spoken word or syllable, a letter or abbreviation, visualized in art or calligraphy, heard chanted by one or more voices in a variety of tones and meter, or symbolized in some other form. In ancient times they were taken from the Sanskrit. One of the most ancient and also most commonly used is OM. This is known as the "sacred syllable," "the Word," "primordial sound," or "the voice of nature or God." It is both a prayer and a chant. Try this experiment: Sitting comfortably, open your mouth and jaw slightly, no more than half an inch. Produce the sound AH-OO-MM as you exhale. It will probably be a low tone, like a moan. Slowly close your mouth while still making the sound.

You've repeated the sacred syllable! AH symbolizes beginning, creation, action that breaks the primordial silence, a call or command to life. OO symbolizes the life force. You shouldn't form the OO with your lips, but sound it only with a slightly open mouth, to emit the sound and feel its resonance. Notice how OO is projected out from you, not produced as deep inside you as the AH sound. MM is the sound of cosmic consciousness or mystic unity. It closes the system, rounds it out, completes the mantra, completes creation. You don't need to intone OM aloud to use it in meditation. You can visualize it in a variety of typefaces, in a variety of forms (sign, flag, rock, book, paper), or imagine it chanted by voices (man, woman, child, chorus, or your own voice). Repeat it, but always slowly. Some choose to hear it with each breath inhaled, each breath exhaled, or both.

Positive Signs

What meditation feels like varies from one person to another. There are, however, certain typical signs of the meditative state. Relaxation is most frequently reported, though the words used to describe it vary: "inner peace," "free-floating calm," "being completely at rest," "getting away from it all," "being out of the body," and so on. Slowed, shallow breathing and some slight slouching are the result of deep relaxation. There can be eyelid flutter or muscle twitching, signs of muscles so "loose" and relaxed there is a random firing of neural impulses. A very good sign, one that often brings a Mona Lisa smile to a yoga practitioner's face, is an invading thought that floats by harmlessly.

Yoga is "alive and well" in the twenty-first century. It has endured for thousands of years and helped millions to better understand and master their minds and bodies. It can do so for you. Open yourself to it and you can increase your self-awareness and achieve self-actualization as well. This is the yogic "yoking" of yourself to the whole universe in a cosmic consciousness. Exploring inner space raises consciousness to a realization of the essence of life. May it be so for you!

Other Lights from the East

What is true anywhere is true everywhere.
Ralph Waldo Emerson, *Conduct of Life* (1860)

LIGHTS FROM CHINA

CONFUCIUS (K'UNG FU TSE)

Confucius is a Latinization of K'ung Fu Tse (pronounced "Koong Foots") or K'ung Ch-iu (pronounced "Koong Joo"), which means "philosopher king." He was born in 551 BCE in Kufow in the state of Lu (now Shantung Province), and died in 479 BCE. He was an avid reader and scholar of history and ancient writings. He moved from place to place, teaching what he considered the basis for a moral and virtuous life. Though he called himself "a transmitter, not a creator," his sayings were collected by followers and became *The Analects*, one of the classics of Chinese literature. He has been called China's "uncrowned emperor" and, with Buddha and Lao Tse, is one of the three great lights of Asia.

K'ung Fu Tse emphasized moral integrity, loyalty, and

compassion. Like Lao Tse, he saw ethics as coming from nature and taught that the virtuous are in harmony with their own nature and with all of nature as well. But his teachings are far more structured than those of Taoism. K'ung Fu Tse's goal was moral social order, while Lao Tse's was mystic unity. They lived at the same time but in different provinces, and there is no evidence they ever met. However, there is a legend that K'ung Fu Tse heard of Lao Tse and wanted to meet him. He sent a messenger to invite him to visit. As soon as the messenger was out of sight an old man approached, riding a donkey. The old man was Lao Tse, who "knew" of the invitation even before it was delivered.

According to that legend, K'ung Fu Tse proudly showed his guest his extensive library. Old Lao Tse smiled and said: "It would be very good on a cold winter night." K'ung Fu Tse was pleased: "Yes, indeed, I spend many hours reading then." Lao Tse replied: "It is far more useful to burn them to keep warm." The legend contrasts these two great thinkers: K'ung Fu Tse, the scholar seeking more and more factual knowledge, and Lao Tse, a mystic seeking more spiritual light. One focused on social action, the other on solitary reflection.

Analects

K'ung Fu Tse's *Lun Yu* (*Analects*) is a collection of writings on a variety of subjects. Here is a sampling:

FROM BOOK 1: The great benefit of rituals is harmony. Ancient leaders saw this. Rituals help in matters small and great. If things go wrong, one who can use rituals to bring harmony can correct them. Things will go wrong without rituals that bring harmony.

FROM BOOK 2: At fifteen I dedicated myself to learning. At thirty I had firm convictions and took my stand. At forty I was self-confident and satisfied. At fifty I knew more about higher values. At sixty I was more perceptive. At seventy I followed my heart and did what was simple and right. Do not preach what you practice until you have practiced what you preach. If you learn but do not think, you are lost; if you think but do not learn, you are in greater trouble. Knowledge is knowing something, both what you know and what you do not know.

FROM BOOK 7: I have transmitted what I was taught without adding anything of my own. I do not have innate knowledge. I love the past and I diligently investigated it.

FROM BOOK 12: Behave when away from home as you would before an important person. Relate to others as carefully as you would conduct an important ceremony. Do not do to others what you would not like done to you. There can then be no bad feelings, either in relations publicly or privately in your family.

FROM BOOK 15: If you see me as one who seeks to learn and remember many things, you are wrong. I have but one way of thinking, on which everything else depends. If there is one thing to guide you every day it is: Never do to others what you would not like them to do to you.

FROM BOOK 16: There are nine ways of caring: seeing clearly, hearing well, being kind, being respectful, speaking truthfully, doing good work, asking questions when in doubt, considering the consequences when angry, and considering what is right when faced with opportunity.

Confucius (K'ung Fu Tse)

—

Feng Shui

Feng Shui (pronounced "Foong Shwee") is an ancient Chinese system of arranging your life and surroundings for maximum spiritual effect. This is accomplished by taking advantage of the flow of *qi*, the life-supporting universal force in Yin-Yang balance of the five basic elements: earth, water, fire, wood, and metal. *Feng* means wind and *shui* is water. This system joins the mystic (unseen moving air) with the more practical and material (water). *Qi* radiates from the dynamic interaction of Yin and Yang, which are equal forces in nature.

As in Taoism, Yin is symbolized by the moon, earth, shade, and repose. It is drawn as two short dashes. Yang ("dragon spirit") is symbolized by the sun, fire, light, heat, action, and activity. It is drawn as one long dash. Arranging the Yin and Yang elements into sets of three lines (trigrams) forms different designs. Four are shown around the red and blue Yin-Yang symbol on the flag of South Korea. Arranging the Yin and Yang elements into six-line figures yields sixty-four different hexagrams, the basis for the *I Ching*.

The five basic elements exist throughout the universe and also can be seen in everyday life. Rounded or flowing objects and "fluid" situations symbolize water. Pointed or erect objects and "hot" situations are fire symbols. Narrow or hard objects and situations are wood, and those that are domed, shiny, or "cold" are metal symbols. Rivers and streams can be viewed in terms of the five elements: sharp turns are fire, narrow or straight running is wood, smooth gently curving rivers symbolize metal, a meandering river is water, and ox-bow lakes formed by an old meandering river that stopped flowing symbolize earth.

The five elements interact in a mystic unity, described by the ancients as rain (water) nourishing forests (wood) used for cooking and comfort (fire) and to refine ore (earth) into metal which, when melted, flows like water, completing the mystic interaction.

In Feng Shui five pairs of divine or heavenly stems represent the five elements. *Jia* and *Yi*, hard and soft, are symbolized as wood. *Bing* and *Ding* represent the types of fire that, respectively, flash in lightning, and burn slowly in incense or charcoal. *Wu* and *Ji* represent earth, whether rocky, as in mountains, or sandy, as on beaches. *Geng* and *Xin* represent metal, finished and wrought or in ores. *Ren* and *Gui* are water forms, seen in rivers, lakes, oceans, raindrops, and snowflakes. These ten stems are applied to compass positions and zodiac birth symbols. *Jia* and *Yi* are tiger and rabbit, and are in the east. *Bing* and *Ding* are dog and ox, at the center. *Geng* and *Xin* are rooster and monkey, in the west. *Ren* and *Gui* are pig and rat, in the north.

The Magic Square

Legends differ about the origin of this interesting table of numbers, sometimes called "the river chart." The most popular legend about its source is that a giant tortoise emerged from the Lo River in about 2000 BCE with the Magic Square on its back. Another legend is it was carried by a half-dragon half-horse that emerged from the Yalu River. Its attention to direction and number show its relationship with traditional Feng Shui. Here it is:

```
        N

     8  1  6
 W   3  5  7   E
     4  9  2

        S
```

Adding the three numbers in any column—whether horizontally, vertically, or diagonally—results in a sum of 15. This feature makes the Magic Square special and powerful. The placement of the numeral 5 in the center gives that number particular significance. The ancients taught that the Magic Square "stands on 9, is 3 to the left and 7 to the right, and has 1 on its head." The numerals 2, 4, 6, and 8 make up the corners. These numerals were often used to design palaces and temples and the number of rooms or stories. The Magic Square was also applied to compass directions. The south, the most favored direction, was seen as 9 (the highest number). The north, the least favored, was considered 1. The west was 3 and the east, 7. The numbers associated with intermediate directions were 6 for northeast; 8 for northwest; 2 for southeast, and 4 for southwest.

Shapes and Forms School

The oldest Feng Shui manual, *The Water Dragon*, is thought to have been written by Yang Yun Sung (ca. CE 600). The Shapes and Forms School also emerged at about this time. This school was based on *qi*, Yin and Yang, the four animals, and five elements. *Qi* is "dragon's breath," or the movement of energy. Good Feng Shui is to have it flow into and through every room. Doors and windows should never be used for the direct, straight-line flow of air. Indirect ventilation allows *qi* to move freely through the house and to be present in every room at all times. The four animals are the green dragon, white tiger, tortoise, and phoenix bird. They symbolize the ideal arrangement of buildings and rooms.

Houses and main entrances should face south (the phoenix bird). The rear should face north with a backdrop (tortoise) of shrubs, trees, higher land, or mountains. The east side is Yin, the green dragon, rising beyond, in a higher building or wall. The west side is Yang, the white tiger, with rolling terrain beyond. Busy streets or highways, entrances, doorways, featured walls, and odd-numbered steps or floors are dragon symbols. Beds should be against a wall (tortoise), not adjacent to a window (tiger or dragon).

Compass School

Wang K'e is credited with founding this school in about CE 1000. It added an astrological and time perspective to Feng Shui, with the Eight-house or Flying Star theories based on the zodiac signs, the twenty-eight constellations, the sixty-four *I Ching* hexagrams, the five Feng Shui elements, Yin and Yang, and *qi*.

Principles School

In about the eleventh century CE, Chu Hsi developed a system based on two factors: principle (*li*), a reflection of the Tai chi Great Ultimate; and *qi*, matter. It was believed that enlightenment depended on increasing *li* and decreasing *qi*. As this process continued, one could become so enlightened as to understand everything.

T'AI CHI CH'UAN

T'ai chi ch'uan, or *T'ai chi*, is a form of the Chinese martial art of *kung fu*, or *wushu*. It was used not only for fighting but also as a meditative exercise or slow form of dance. Its origin is uncertain but estimates range from 1000 to 250 BCE. As a philosophy Tai chi seeks mystic unity of Yin with Yang and the basic five elements of water, wood, fire, earth, and metal. The Yin-Yang symbol also symbolizes Tai chi but adds the eight basic *I Ching* hexagrams around the basic Yin-Yang circle.

The Tai chi ritual is a systematic, stylized, slow-motion form of exercise using body movements originally used in combat. It was believed that principle (*li*) began the process of creation, and that matter (*chi*, which is an alternative pronunciation of *qi*) resulted from it. The ritual repeats this process, achieving mystic unity of Yin and Yang and the five basic elements within the individual. Tai chi is still widely practiced throughout China.

FALUN DAFA, FALUN GONG

Falun Dafa ("wheel of law") and *Falun Gong* (pronounced "Faloon Goong": "the way of body, mind, and spirit energy") are ancient Chinese practices based on five exercises done in special body positions with hand movements, usually accompanied by music. Three of the exercises are mainly physical and two are meditative.

Li Honghzhi, or Master Li, has recently emerged as the movement's leader, although many involved in the movement consider a leader unnecessary. Though no total membership figures are maintained, estimates run as high as seventy million Chinese and thirty million others outside China. If accurate, this number exceeds the membership of China's Communist Party. In 1999, Falun Gong was declared illegal in China amid claims by the authorities that it was a harmful cult spreading superstition and destructive political activism. Adherents claim that the movement is "a way of life," and not a cult or a religion.

Falung Gong incorporates elements from Feng Shui, Buddhism, and Taoism, and adds an emphasis on *qi-gong* (pronounced "Chee Goong"). *Qi*, as we have seen, is the universal life force; *gong* is the way to develop it. As Buddha required, it is a volunteer movement with members free to come, go, or return. There are no paid staff, dues, fees, or entrance requirements. Its symbol is a swastika that bears no relationship with Hitler's Nazism. The swastika is an ancient symbol used in India, China, the Middle East, and Teutonic Europe, and by pre-Colombian Native Americans. It is seen as revolving, absorbing energy clockwise and radiating energy counterclockwise.

KAKUAN'S BULL

Kuoan Shiyuan (Kakuan Shien in Japanese) was a twelfth-century Chinese Ch'an (Zen) master. He used finding and taming a bull as a metaphor for spiritual enlightenment. This is a ten-step sequence, each step beginning with a statement from the person seeking enlightenment followed by Kakuan's advice and teaching. Enlightenment comes from mastering each step.

1. The Bull Is Missing

On my path of life it is as if I search through tall grass to find the bull. I search uncharted rivers and crossroads to distant mountains. I tire and cannot find the bull.

KAKUAN'S ADVICE: The bull was never lost! You are lost, separated from your true self and your transcendent nature. Your search fails because you are unaware of this. Your usual senses and skills do not help, but weaken you and lead you to feel lost and alone and to believe that the bull is missing. Without enlightenment it will get worse.

2. Here, Tracks

Here, tracks on the riverbank!
And here, more tracks in the grass!
They are as clear as the nose on my face.

KAKUAN'S ADVICE: You do not see the bull, but only see outward signs that something was there. There is more to life than what you know. With greater awareness you will see the bull and not just the signs left behind. You must choose: will you see what is there, or what you wish to see? This is how you got into trouble.

3. Stop, Be Alert

Resting from the search I hear a bird singing.
The sun is warm, the wind mild, and the trees green.
I still cannot see the bull. It's not here.

KAKUAN'S ADVICE: You see and hear much more when you do not try so hard. The green trees calm the day without your seeking it. The bird's song and the soft breeze add to the night's calm. They appear and speak for themselves, stronger together than each alone, as if two and two are five. Use your thoughts and senses this same way. You will improve your awareness and open the way to the bull.

4. Fight It, Catch It

A gate opens and I wrestle with the bull.

Strong and stubborn, it runs away.
I'm high above the clouds on a steep cliff.

KAKUAN'S ADVICE: You made contact, but only for a short time. The bull goes where it will, according to its nature. It knows the territory better than you. You wander about according to your nature. The fact that you made contact shows that you are more aware than before, but the bull's escape shows that you must improve further.

5. Tame It

I found the bull and tamed it, but still it runs away.
If I can understand its nature I can tame it more.
Then it will stay with me and won't want to run away.

KAKUAN'S ADVICE: Good. Be open to what is and what is not. Let beings be. Simplify. Busy minds use much time and energy. Overdo, and you will be so full that what is important cannot get in. Always start by letting everything be what it is, according to its own nature. Forcing anything violates it and leads to evil and delusion. Open up to yourself and find your own true way.

6. Ride It

I ride the bull and play the flute.
We keep time in harmony.
Is anyone listening? Come join us.

KAKUAN'S ADVICE: As long as you, the bull, and anyone else are open to their true natures there can be harmony. Feelings of failure or loss are then less relevant and less troubling. Being aware of and doing this is to sing the song of the birds, animals, fish, and children everywhere. Few hear it.

7. Transcend It

The bull and I arrive home.
We rest together quietly.
There is no need to do anything.

KAKUAN'S ADVICE: Knowing that there is one nature shared by all living things brings the calm of deep inner peace. Then there is no need to strain against obstacles. Everything flows by its nature and all is well.

8. Transform Yourself

Differences fade by sharing openly and truthfully.
The universe is vast, wonderful, and free.
It is enlightening to follow this path.

KAKUAN'S ADVICE: When differences are seen as trivial and unimportant there is no conflict. Differences emerge of and by themselves and there is no need to act for or against them, or to form or reform them. This makes it difficult for anyone to know you, since neither praise nor scorn have any real meaning. Knowing that no one owns anything or anyone brings harmony to relationships. Perception is clear and limitless and the path onward and upward is well lighted.

9. Realize the Source

It has taken a long time for me to awaken.
It would be easier to be blind and deaf.
To live naturally is like being a blossoming flower.

KAKUAN'S ADVICE: Truth and wisdom never change, from beginning to end. It takes time to realize this. Enlightenment is silent. Do not seek it, and you will have it. Ignore it, and it is still there. Mountains, valleys, oceans, and rivers are created and destroyed naturally, because of their own natures.

10. Transcend!

I interact as if naked before everyone and everything.
I am poor yet rich and happy. I need no magic to live
longer or better. To me even the dead are alive.

KAKUAN'S ADVICE: If you have reached this step you can now say: "I am unknown. My garden is beautiful, even if only to me. I need not search for enlightenment elsewhere. I work, walk the streets, and return home, and anyone else can freely share in this enlightenment."

LIGHTS FROM JAPAN

SHINTO

Shinto is written with the characters for "god" and "way" and is most frequently translated as "the way of the gods," meaning the spiritual force or divine spirit (*kami*) that resides in everything: animals, birds, people, or objects such as rocks, flowers, and water. Shinto is among the world's oldest religions and Japan's own nature-based religion. Shintoists share the same deep reverence for nature as China's Taoists.

Its origins are lost in antiquity but it has been traced back to about 1000 BCE. It emerged in the sixth century CE but its roots are deep in the folk religions of Korea, Manchuria, and

Siberia. According to Shinto tradition Emperor Jinmu founded Japan in 660 BCE; this emperor was believed to be descended directly from the sun goddess Amaterasu Omikami. As time passed, the areas of overlap between Shinto and Buddhism increased until now neighboring Shinto shrines and Buddhist temples are sometimes affiliated, and most Japanese now take part in rituals associated with one or the other tradition as custom dictates. Shinto is associated with happy occasions and Buddhism with life after death; accordingly, in general, traditional Japanese weddings are Shinto, and traditional Japanese funerals are Buddhist.

Ryobu ("two kinds") Shinto emerged at the end of the eighth century, blending Shinto with Buddhism and Confucian ethics. Yearning for a distinctively Japanese religion led to the Meiji Restoration in 1868 when Shinto became the state religion and was taught in the schools. Belief in divine succession and teaching Shinto in schools ended in 1945 with Japan's defeat in World War II.

Shinto Today

Shinto continues to be practiced throughout Japan at public shrines and at shrines in homes, at roadsides, in gardens, parks, and seashores, and at public festivals. There, prayers and offerings are given for the *kami* spirit of the place. It is estimated there are more than three million Shintoists in Japan served by one hundred thousand Shinto priests in eighty thousand shrines. There are special rituals and festivals that mark life stages and natural events. There is the 7-5-3 (*shichi-go-san*) festival when five-year-old boys and three-year-old and seven-year-old girls are taken to shrines for good health. Every shrine also has its own annual festival.

More than ten million Japanese participate in Shinto rituals but less than a third identify themselves as Shintoists. Such is the power of its tradition of fellow feeling and reverence for nature. Typical Shinto prayers and rituals ask for good health, happiness, peace, and success. The distinctive symbol of Shinto is the *torii*, a tall wooden gateway with a distinctive curved lintel. Walking through it, one is thought to leave the outside world and enter the world of the *kami* spirit of that place. Like ancient Greek temples of Asklepios, Shinto sites are usually in serene settings near greenery, earth forms such as hills or rock, and still water. One interesting Shinto object is the *kamidana*, an altar or household shrine, ideally made of *hinoki* wood, and sometimes with a mirror of the gods (*shinkyo*).

There is no single all-powerful God in Shinto, though Nature holds a central place and is its major focus. Earthquakes, flood, and fires are seen as aspects of divine *kami* force. Shinto has no scripture like the Judeo-Christian Bible or Islamic Qu'ran. There is no required catechism and no rigid dogma, but there are two major writings: *Kojiki* (The record of ancient matters), and *Nihongi* (The chronicles of Japan), both of which combine records of ancient Japanese historical matters with Shinto myth and legend.

Major Shinto sects focus on a specific mission such as preserving the ancient ways, faith healing, purification rites, Confucian ethics, or reverence for nature, especially mountains. There are lesser Shinto sects, founded by individuals and continued by followers. There are four basic "affirmations" for all Shintoists: reverence for nature; cleanliness of body and spirit; respect for family and tradition; and fellowship in sharing with others such as in rituals and at festivals.

THE WAY OF THE SAMURAI AND MUSASHI'S *FIVE RINGS*

Miyamoto Musashi, also known as Shinmen Musashi, was a famous sixteenth-century Japanese swordsman/philosopher/ artist/teacher known as *kensei*, or "the sword saint." He is remembered for his swordsmanship and teachings on strategy in *Gorinsho*, or *The Book of Five Rings*, written just before his death at age sixty. His teachings would have been read by samurai, who were dedicated to a strict code of Shinto-Zen chivalry and *kendo*, or "the way of the sword." According to legend, Musashi was thirteen when he first defeated a samurai, a phenomenal achievement if true. He went on to win many duels, although instead of killing opponents he preferred to use a wooden sword, eluding his opponent's blade, and inflicting serious blows with his ingenuity and quick moves. He fought in the Ashigara-Ieyasu War where an estimated seventy thousand were killed in three days.

As Musashi aged he spent less time in swordfighting and more in meditation, painting, wood sculpture, and fine metalwork. He said he didn't really understand strategy until he was fifty. In his later years he lived alone in a cave where just before his death in CE 1645 he wrote *The Book of Five Rings*. He began the book with "the way of strategy." It is said that he chose his words as carefully as he chose his combat tactics. Musashi, aging and alone, realized that his life was at its end and he took time to meditate and finely craft his message. His term "the way of strategy" suggests the five rings are as much a meditative system as a skilled old soldier's advice on war. Here are excerpts from the *Book of Five Rings*:

The Way of Strategy

"Master swordsmen are not just warriors. The way of strategy comes from the gods. The four classes of people use it in their own way: farmers to plan, plant, and produce; merchants to select, store, and sell; craftsmen to master and skillfully use materials; and warriors to master and skillfully use weapons. All these first plan what is to be done, know the underlying principles that apply, carefully choose the men and materials needed, and fashion a plan to achieve success.

"To learn the way of strategy, reflect on all this and adopt it as your way. Doing so means that when you overcome one thing you can overcome all things. Avoid a favorite weapon; know them all. Develop and master your own style; do not emulate or copy others. Time and timing are important and require much practice. There are in all five rings of my way of strategy. They vary with the importance of the situation and your ingenuity. You succeed by knowing your own timing and that of others, and by using this in unexpected ways."

First Ring: Grounding—Rooting

Musashi recommended carefully building a foundation on which to grow, by formal education, career training, moral teachings of Buddha, Confucius, or a religion of your choice, and "many arts and skills." This foundation should be physical and mental, "the way of the warrior" (physical) and "the way of the pen" (mental). He listed nine rules. "Set your heart firmly on them, study them diligently and you will know much more."

1. Be honest.

2. Train and master the way; maintain proficiency.

The Way
of the
Samurai
and
Musashi's
Five
Rings
—
143

3. Be familiar with all the arts.

4. Be familiar with the ways of the professions.

5. Know the difference between winning and losing, usefulness and uselessness.

6. Develop intuition and higher awareness.

7. See the unseen.

8. Focus on details—the incidental and the important.

9. Do nothing that is not necessary.

His instructions: "This book is a spiritual guide. Read and reflect on it word for word. Read it too quickly or too superficially and you will lose your way. Read and fail to absorb it and you will fail miserably."

Second Ring: Humble as Water

"To master this ring you must become as water. Water takes the shape of the container; so you should adjust to the realities of the situation. Water flows according to its volume, in a trickle or a torrent; so you should apply yourself according to the needs of the situation. Water is clear and you should be as clear in your expectations and directions. Knowing this is to know ten thousand things.

"Be steadfast, determined but calm. Meet situations openly, body ready but mind relaxed. Do not let your mind relax your body. Do not let the enemy see into your mind. Superiors should know the minds of inferiors but strive to be high-minded nevertheless. You will know you have achieved the Way of Strategy when no one can deceive you.

"Be and look upright, head erect, brow unwrinkled, eyes open and aware, body balanced and centered. This is your combat posture. Perceive more than you see and do not be distracted or misled. See to either side while looking ahead. Use this daily in every situation, major or minor.

"Use weapons, tools, and materials as if they are part of you. Develop Yin-Yang *feet*, neither preferred nor stronger, both equal. In every situation be aware of the *five aspects*: left, right, high, low, and middle. Middle is the center and strongest aspect. To live *the way of the sword* means to always use the five aspects. *One-timing* is taking action or solving a problem quickly, decisively, in one stroke. *Body 1-2* means to feign a first move followed by a decisive second blow.

Third Ring: Living Fire

Fire symbolized action "the same for one battle or ten thousand battles" and Musashi urged constant practice so that when action is actually needed it can be performed as easily as one's "daily routine." The translation continues:

"Place yourself in the most advantageous location and position. Keep the enemy moving and limit his awareness of his position. There are three basic actions: attacking, repelling, and locking. Attacking is best, but to win you must know the enemy's mind and strategy. Attack quickly but calmly. To defend, then repel, feign weakness and then counterattack forcefully when the enemy shows confusion or slows down. When locked in combat, continue to attack calmly, moving in through weak points. *Holding down the pillow* is encouraging the enemy's useless actions and discouraging or defeating actions that can hurt you. *River crossing* is finding the enemy's weak point then taking action against it as you would cross a river; this is also important in life, as you chart your life's course though others stay ashore, and find your way across life's river, even rowing when the wind is not favorable. *Enjoining* is defeating one strong

The Way
of the
Samurai
and
Musashi's
Five
Rings
—
145

point after another like walking along a winding path.

"*Stepping on the sword* means defeating an enemy totally, in body and mind, preventing counterattack, and remaining on alert afterward. *Penetration* is demoralizing the enemy as well as overcoming him. *Crushing* is defeating the enemy so totally that he is deprived of all resources. *Becoming the enemy* is thinking as your enemy thinks, to better understand his plans and likely responses. *Time testing* is closely observing what is happening and when, and then using the enemy's timetable against him. *Being unpredictable* and *doing the unexpected* adds to the effect. *Four hands* is a situation in which you and the enemy are deadlocked. In this case, do the unexpected. *Passing it on* is feigning adjusting to the enemy's strategy and then, just when he adjusts to your actions, suddenly changing strategy, and attacking. *Soaking in* means assuming the same strategy as the enemy, to better understand his weaknesses.

"*Fear tactics* are upsetting the enemy by making a small force or action seem much larger, or feigning that you are more upset than you really are. *Chaos* is keeping the enemy confused by constantly changing tactics. The *mountain-sea* tactic is never using the same tactic twice. *Three yells* refers to shouting three times during combat: at the start, during the fight, and at the end to proclaim victory. *Rat-head ox-neck* is being able to shift quickly from one different tactic to another and from minor details to major points. *Letting go* is deliberate inaction and to win without a sword. *Being a rock* is total commitment to the Way of Strategy."

Fourth Ring: Changing Winds

To Musashi, the variety of beliefs and traditions are winds of change. He recommended studying all of them to see "the

Way in all of them." In his words: "Winds blow from many directions, weak and strong, and often change. So it is with theories and beliefs, methods and materials. Being aware of this diversity yet understanding the underlying principle is to see 'the Way' in all of them. Not being aware of this limits you only to what you yourself know and believe, a narrow path in only one direction."

Musashi wrote: "Most ways are not the Way of Strategy but the Way of Strategy is in all ways. Some are narrow and some are wide. Some are strong and others are weak. Some overdo, others underdo. Some emphasize eyes or feet, others emphasize speed or secret teachings. To win you must use the enemy's weakness. That requires that you know the various ways of all enemies."

Fifth Ring: No-Thing

This fifth and last step is the Zen "mystic leap" of being so open that you have no bias, no preconceived notion, no fixed belief. Your mind is not in motion and is open to whatever is there, not to what you want, expect, fear, or need. The previous four rings forge this last one, a high ground aware of everything and everyone, obvious and hidden, here, everywhere, nowhere. He described this ring as being aware "without beginning or end," open to "the way and power of nature."

Musashi wrote: "If you know what exists you know what does not exist, the void. Many think that what is not understood is the void. This is not so. To know the Way of Strategy you must intently study the other ways. It settles the mind and by daily practice the two-level mind of thinking and feeling is refined and there is two-level envisioning by sensing and perceiving. Clouds of uncertainty will pass, leaving the void. Fixed beliefs, rigid systems, and believing all is well is not the Way of Strategy. The Way is in the void where there is truth without error, virtue without evil, and wisdom beyond mind."

HAIKU

A haiku is a brief poem of seventeen syllables. It has been popular in Japan for centuries and like Asian art it depicts the beauty of nature and touching moments of reverie. Here is a sampling of the haiku of Basho (Matsuo Munefusa, CE 1644–94), who was one of Japan's most famous poets:

Basho's Haiku

For a lovely bowl
let us arrange these
flowers since there is no rice.

Take the round flat moon
snap a twig handle.
What a pretty fan it is.

Here where a thousand
captains won battles
tall grass is their monument.

Why so scrawny, cat?
Longing for a fish,
a mouse, or just backyard love?

Haiku of Others

First dream of the year.
I kept it secret,
smiling only to myself. (Sho-u)

Brightly colored stones
vibrate in the creek ——
or maybe it's the water. (Soseki)

> I must turn over.
> Beware of local
> earthquakes, bedfellow cricket. (Issa)

Live in simple faith
just as the trusting
cherry flowers, fades, and falls. (Issa)

> When they ask for me
> say: "He had some
> business in another world." (Sokan)

Riverbank plum tree
do your reflected
blossoms really flow away? (Buson)

> Now wild geese return.
> What draws them crying,
> Crying all the long dark night? (Roka)

A childless housewife,
how tenderly she
touches little dolls for sale. (Ransetsu)

> Ashes, my burnt hut,
> but wonderful the
> cherry blooming on my hill. (Hokushi)

I scooped up the moon
in my water pail
but I spilled it on the grass. (Ryuko)

> Pretty butterflies!
> Be careful of the pine
> Needle points in the strong wind. (Shusen)

On the last long road
when I fall for good
I will sleep with the flowers. (Sora)

LIGHT FROM TIBET

The Tibetan Book of the Dead

More than a thousand years ago, high in the Himalayas, Tibetan
lamas taught how to travel from death to a new life. *Bardo Thodol*,
or *The Tibetan Book of the Dead*, is in content and style part of
Tantric Buddhism, more esoteric and mystic than Hinayana or
Mahayana Buddhism. Tibetan Buddhists believe if you cannot
achieve enlightenment in this life it is still possible to achieve it
during the three *bardo* (Sanskrit for "stage") of death, a forty-
nine-day period. Dying is the first stage, the *chikhai bardo*. The
second is *chonyid bardo*, a drifting, dreamlike stage. *Sidpa bardo* is
the third and final stage, that of prebirth. The book was read
aloud by the living to the dead, to help them find their way to
rebirth. Here are excerpts from each *bardo*, with a sampling of
typical prayers.

The Guide

With these teachings Buddhahood can be achieved at the time
of your death. Buddhahood can be achieved by hearing, remembering, meditating on, and knowing these teachings and what
happens after death. If you know these teachings at the time of
your death you will be saved from a long and painful journey.
If you do not know them listen carefully now. The sights and
sounds you will experience will come to you regardless of your
religion and the extent to which you practiced it. Accept and

absorb the teachings and you will be liberated as soon as your consciousness and body separate. This is the Great Liberation. Even the most sinful can be liberated if they hear, remember, meditate on, and know them and what happens after death. If difficult for you, you can be liberated just by not disbelieving them.

Instructions

Read these teachings to everyone, to the sick, the dying, and the dead. Study them, meditate on them, and know them. Even if you hear them only once or do not fully understand them you will remember and understand them in the *bardo*, because there memory is nine times better. After death these teachings should be read to you by the guru who taught you. If this is not possible, a brother or learned man of the same faith should read them. If this is not possible, a person who speaks clearly should read. During the reading there should be silence and no weeping. If there is no body the reader should lie in your bed or sit in your chair. Your spirit will be there. If there is a body, when death comes the reader should speak clearly into your ear. An offering should be made of what is available. Pleasant incense should be burned. These teachings are read three or seven times each of the forty-nine days of the *bardo* journey. The first reading should be before death—before the heart stops, the lungs give up vital force, and the mind no longer recognizes earthly things. The book from which these teachings are read to you should be buried or burned with your body.

Chikhai Bardo

You may have heard these words before but do not know that you are dead. You may know you are dead but not understand it. Concentrate now and remember the words you are now hearing and you can see the Primary Clear Light. You do not have to go through the three *bardo* planes if you accept these teachings, earnestly search for truth, and combine them with good karma. Do this and you will be on the Great Upward Path.

Invocation

Buddhas and bodhisattvas here and everywhere, all-knowing, all-seeing, all-loving, all-protecting, come now to one in need. Compassionate Ones, wise and understanding, powerful, protective, and infinite, please be advised that (name of deceased) is passing from worldly existence. It is a great change and (name) is in great need of help and enlightenment. (He/she) is falling, unprotected, deeper into the void surrounded by karmic forces. (He/she) is anxious and afraid and needs strength to go on. Compassionate Ones, help the helpless, defend the defenseless, protect the unprotected. Be (her/his) help and strength. Save (name) from fear, evil karmic forces, and from a long and painful *bardo*. Let your power and love flow freely. This is asked with sincerity, humility, and deep faith.

First Prayer

Buddhas, fathers of the way, divine mothers, here and everywhere, brothers and sisters of the way, now and from all ages past, gurus, gods, spirits, the multitude of the faithful, listen with love and compassion and give help along the way.

Second Prayer

When we in this life, in this world, wander from the path of enlightenment may the Buddhas and gurus, all-knowing fathers, inspire and strengthen us. May the divine mothers comfort and support us. May we be spared a long and painful *bardo*. May we achieve Buddhahood.

Tenth Prayer

May we be welcomed in the Eastern Realm by Aksobhya, the Blue Buddha; may we be welcomed in the Southern Realm by Ratnasambhava, the Yellow Buddha; may we be welcomed in the Western Realm by Amithaba, the Red Buddha; may we be welcomed in he Northern Realm by Amoghassidhi, the Green Buddha; may we be welcomed in the Central Realm by Vairocana, the White Buddha; may we be welcomed in all the realms so that we can join with all the Buddhas. May *bardo* sights and sounds be our sights and sounds. May we see, accept, and join the Tri-kaya, Dharma-kaya mystic unity; Sambhoga-kaya wisdom; and Nirmana-kaya enlightenment.

Twenty-fourth Prayer

When it is time for me to be reborn may I be free from evil. When I am born according to my wish may it be free of bad karma.

Twenty-seventh Prayer

When I first see my future parents may I see them as Divine Mother-Father. When I choose rebirth may I have Buddha qualities.

Thirtieth Prayer

In learning tasks and duties may I understand and learn quickly; may all be well wherever I am born and may all I contact be happy.

Final Prayer

May my motives and intentions be as pure as I earnestly want them to be; may everyone everywhere achieve Buddhahood; may enlightenment spread throughout the world; may these teachings be used well by all; may virtue and goodness grow and grow, forever and ever.

Chonyid Bardo

(This is the bardo of terrifying karmic illusions seen and heard by the deceased. It was believed that it takes three-and-a-half days to realize that you are dead. The spirit of the deceased cannot be seen or heard by anyone. For fourteen days the deceased was called by name and instructed with these words.)

Listen carefully with undivided attention. There are six *bardo* states, three involved with life and three involved with death. The first *bardo* state is being in the womb awaiting birth. The second is the dream-state. The third is experiencing mystic unity. The fourth is *chikhai bardo*, the moment of death. The fifth is *chonyid bardo*, karmic illusions after death. The sixth is *sidpa bardo*, seeking rebirth. You have already passed through *chikhai bardo*. The Primary Clear Light shone but you could not see it or be one with it, so you are now in *chonyid bardo*. Listen carefully. You are dead and it is time to leave this world. You do this alone but know that death comes to all and others have passed this way before. Do not cling to life because of longing or fear of going on. You do not have the power to remain here and there is no value in aimless wandering. Think about this teaching and the Compassionate Buddha from whence it comes. Meditate thus:

"When karmic illusions dawn upon me and fear and terror rise in me may I realize they are from within me, a natural part of the *bardo* of death. May I realize good and evil karmic illusions are my own."

Sidpa Bardo

(This third and final stage instructs the deceased on how to seek rebirth. On the fifteenth day the sidpa bardo *was read to the deceased.)*

You did not become one with the deities in the *chonyid bardo* so you are now in the *sidpa bardo*. Birth here is not like on earth. Remember, you did not know you were dead and then your consciousness changed, like a fish jumping from the water. Your *bardo* self seems like your human self but it is more perfect, positive, with signs of what is to come. If you keep your consciousness clear and positive you can be liberated without entering the womb. If you cannot do this, meditate on your guru or favorite deity and see it as a crown on your head. No longer in your human form, you can now move freely in every way, even through houses and mountains. You can change size or shape. You can now see and be seen by *bardo* beings—the gods and those with whom you will share your next life. This proves that you are in *sidpa bardo*. Accept it.

You can see and hear humans but they cannot see or hear you. Seeing loved ones causes great pain, like a fish jumping out of water into a fire. For one to seven weeks, depending on your karma, you will be in grey-white light. The wind of karma is behind you, pushing you. Do not fear it. Darkness, screams, and threats lie ahead. Do not fear these, as they come from within you. Bad karma brings demons, wild animals, enraged mobs, and natural disasters, your misdeeds made real. If you flee you will be on a cliff above three valleys of anger, selfishness, and stupidity, further proof that you are in *sidpa bardo*.

Whatever happens, do not be distracted. Your consciousness may dim and you may feel hopeless. Meditate to keep your consciousness clear. You cannot eat, but you can absorb spiritual strength offered to you. You will see your home, loved ones, even your own dead body. You will be sad, wish for, and seek rebirth but be patient and maintain clear consciousness.

* * *

The text continues with instructions to "speak the truth with sincerity and faith" at a last judgment joined by two spirits of the same age and gender as the deceased. One spirit counts the deceased's good deeds and the other counts the evil deeds. If the deceased should lie, the Lord of Death will "chop off your head, tear out your heart, pull out your intestines, eat your brain, drink your blood, chew your flesh and gnaw at your bones." This is repeated if needed! All this "arises from your own thoughts" and is "self-inflicted." Karmic rebirths can end in *nibbana* (nirvana): "Even if you have not recognized anything 'til now you can attain liberation by meditation and praying to Buddha." With prayer "remembering comes, then recognition, acceptance, at-oneness, and final liberation."

At the end of this stage, it was believed, the deceased would see lights "from six worlds of existence, the brightest being your next existence." The text continues, "You will see continents on which you could be born and you should choose one where religion is strong. You will know the proper womb by a pleasant smell. You enter it by concentrating—just as one controls a horse by pulling on the reins—on good elevating thoughts, without distraction. You should do so with love and faith, thus transforming the womb into a holy temple." A "bad womb" may appear good but "those skilled by meditation are free to judge wisely." The *sidpa bardo* ends with a final plea: "Be one with these special teachings and Buddhahood can be achieved. Past, present, and future Buddhas cannot transcend these teachings. The bardo that liberate the dead are now complete."

Tibetan Buddhists traditionally believe in Buddhas of the cardinal directions. In the north is Amoghasiddhi Tara, the Buddha of all-achieving wisdom, fearlessness, decisiveness, and will power, symbolized by a harpy (winged monster), clear air, and a green color field. In the south is Ratnasambhava Mamaki, the Buddha of all-embracing wisdom, charity, humanity, and equality, symbolized by a horse, earth, and yellow. In the West is Amithaba Pandaravashi, the Buddha of discriminating wisdom, receptivity, unmet needs, and convictions, symbolized by a peacock, fire, and red. In the East is Aksobhya Locana, the Buddha of reflective wisdom—wisdom of the great mirror—symbolized by an elephant and flute, water, and white. In the center is Vairocana Akasadhatis, the Buddha of universal consciousness, transcendence, and transformation, symbolized by a wheel and lion, ethereal space, and blue.

The Plains Indians of North America used a similar system: a white buffalo of wisdom in the north, green mouse of innocence in the south, yellow eagle of enlightenment in the east, black bear of introspection in the west, and medicine wheel in the center.

Years ago I gave a talk to school counselors on "current therapies in the ancient East" and included brief descriptions of these ideas. Afterward, a Cherokee medicine man who had been in the audience came up to talk to me. With a broad smile and much enthusiasm he mentioned how moved he was to hear of traditions in distant countries that had such similar imagery.

8
"Orient" Yourself!

Meditation is the breeze that
comes through an open window.
Krishnamurti, *Think on These Things* (1975)

Meditation is one of the most used and most useful methods to achieve spiritual enlightenment. There are many different ways to approach meditation but the most common is to meditate daily for fifteen to twenty minutes in a relaxing quiet place without interruption. Many people have a special place to meditate, a kind of personal temple. It can be a corner of a room or a small space at a shelf or on a side table. Some find incense, soft music, or candlelight helpful. I once asked an old Buddhist monk what he would recommend as most conducive to meditation. His answer: "How about right here, now?" You can meditate anywhere, at any time, but most people prefer to be alone in a quiet place.

There are body positions that are especially conducive to meditative awareness. One of the most common is a seated position with legs and arms crossed. It need not be the lotus position of yoga, which many people find uncomfortable. The object is to focus the attention, then empty the mind, to achieve serenity and higher consciousness. This is hard to do if you are physically tense or in pain.

DEVELOPING MEDITATIVE AWARENESS

The first step in further developing meditative awareness is to have an open mind, much like a child eager and curious for a new adventure. Your journey through your own inner space can be as adventurous as an astronaut exploring outer space. Inscribed over the entrance of ancient Greek was the statement "only the pure in heart may enter here." It was a reminder to seekers of higher truth to "clean up their act." Zen masters have asked: "How much baggage do you carry?" Some have told novices: "Leave your baggage outside." These are examples of applying deeper mystic meanings in everyday conversation and daily living. Having an open mind also involves expecting nothing. No attention should be given to cost or benefit. That is the beginning of selflessness.

Westerners have a bad habit of expecting a "fast-food" experience from meditation. You can't buy (or sell) meditative awareness, mystic insight, or wisdom. The flower opens of and by itself, nurtured by nature and its nature. In Zen terms, "don't push the river." The river of your mind can be blocked by impatience. Go with its natural flow, the flow of nature, not just your nature.

Dictionaries define meditation as "deep, continued thought, concentration, reflection, or contemplation." Meditation is usually associated with religious devotion, but it need not be. Like mysticism, meditation is difficult to describe in words since it is a psychological state and a spiritual process. A beautiful sunrise or sunset or a moving story or piece of music can be a mystic and a meditative experience. Two people can see and hear the same thing but perceive it differently. It is mystic if it "points you" to a higher power or connects with it, best achieved by regular meditation.

Meditation is an altered state of consciousness that has been described as descending into a well that is within you and also as an elevator to a higher floor of awareness. It differs from prayer that asks for help or sends a message. Meditation is more a connection and prayer is more a conversation. Many mental health professionals recommend meditation for its calming effect. It supplements, but does not supplant, psychotherapy.

Daily Routine

Find one item in the daily newspaper that to you is inspiring because it involves a higher level of spiritual or meditative awareness. It may be in a news story, an ad, a photo, or anything. Remember, what to you is inspiring may not be so to others. Spiritual development is an individual process. Try to find something in your daily activities that to you is not "business as usual" but involves higher values or a higher level of consciousness.

Imagined Peaceful Place

Every night, as you lie in bed ready to fall asleep, imagine your own special, peaceful place. You must be there alone, so that you are not distracted by a social relationship. It is necessary for you to be alone, since this facilitates spiritual growth, which is an individual process. It should not be a real place or else you will remember times and people there that interfere with meditative awareness. It should be a safe, relaxing, special place just for you. Consider a mountaintop cabin, a hut on an ocean beach, a beautiful garden, a boat on a calm river, or any scene that you find calming. Every night, picture that same scene as you fall asleep. Take a long, slow, deep breath to help you relax. Don't actively fight invading thoughts but instead focus on details in your scene. That will strengthen the imagery and weaken interrupting thoughts.

Mini-vacations

During the day, occasionally picture your peaceful scene. Do this by closing your eyes for a few seconds and taking a deep breath (not while driving or doing anything that requires close attention, of course). Good times to do this include: as you sit at the table before the first bite of breakfast; at your desk when you arrive for work; just after lunch; on the bus, subway, train, or plane; when you arrive at home, before you get out of the car; in the bathroom; while getting dressed and undressed. Doing this strengthens your before-sleep imagery of your peaceful place and gives you the added advantage of being able to relax in what can sometimes be stressful situations. At such times, just picture your peaceful place and take a little deeper breath than usual. No one will notice but you'll feel a calming effect, as if you had actually spent a few moments in your peaceful place.

Mini-meditation

After you have performed the steps outlined above, try lying on your back in bed or on the floor, legs parted slightly, arms at your sides but not touching, palms up, and a pillow under your head. This is called "the corpse pose" in asana yoga. Get a tape recorder that automatically clicks off at the end of a tape (most do). Use a thirty-minute tape (that means fifteen minutes on each side). Record the sound from a blank TV channel. It sounds like surf, but be sure that there's no music or speech in the background. This is most like "white sound" and is conducive to deep relaxation. Ideally once a day, at a quiet time when you will not be interrupted, lie down and start the tape, adjusting it to a pleasant volume (maximum bass helps). You may want to disconnect the phone. Again picture the scene that you visit each night. You will have fifteen minutes of meditation in your peaceful place. When the tape player clicks off the white sound stops. Don't get up right away, but linger a bit and enjoy the afterglow of relaxation, remembering that you can go to your peaceful place any time, day or night, and use it to pace yourself and cope with your everyday life.

BUDDHA'S METHOD

Buddha taught that meditation could be done at any time of day, for up to half an hour, in a quiet place. The setting should be peaceful, in a quiet or specially prepared place, indoors or outdoors. Buddha was born and raised Hindu and used a yoga position in which he sat upright with legs crossed and folded, the body forming a pyramid. He did not stress a need for the full lotus position. All that is necessary is a stable, balanced posture. The object is to be comfortable enough to focus attention without discomfort, but not so comfortable as to fall asleep.

Buddhist meditation can be described in terms of two states of concentration, known as "steady-state" meditation (*samatha-bhavana*) and "insight" meditation (*vipassana-bhanava*). Steady-state meditation involves focusing the attention on one thing (one-pointed concentration). For example, a color, flame, water, or body function such as breathing, or the five hindrances (ill will, anxiety, sloth, doubt, and sensual desire). Signs of achieving this meditative state are feelings of serenity, freedom, and rapture. Insight meditation is more intense concentration on a specific perception. For example, if breathing is the subject, meditation focuses on every aspect such as the air before, during, and after a breath, the passage of air through the nostrils to the lungs, and the sense of becoming one with it. Steady-state leads to insight meditation and insight meditation depends on steady-state.

Buddha recommended various ways that one can approach meditation.

Body Meditation

With eyes closed, be aware of your breathing, in and out, regularly and relaxed. Notice every aspect of sensation. It may seem strange at first but it helps develop deeper insight meditation. Body meditation should be practiced daily. Use it when awakening in the morning and at bedtime. Everyday activities offer ways to "body meditate." Reflect on what you are doing. Even with eyes open meditative awareness can be developed looking at a peaceful scene, a picture on the wall, a carpeted floor, draperies, furniture, even a desktop. Silent self-talk can help. At any time, pause for a few moments and express awareness of what you're doing. Develop a sensitivity to touch, warmth, pressure, and their effects.

Sight

Focus the attention on what you are seeing using the body meditation method just described ("I am looking at ... ").

Taste

The Japanese tea ceremony is a good example of the use of taste as an object of meditation. Eating more slowly helps develop meditative awareness to taste, texture, temperature, and smell. Fully experience what is happening. Name the sensation: bland, tangy, or spicy; sweet, bitter, or sour; warm or cold.

Fragrance

Focus the attention on the sense of smell. Be aware of smells, good and bad. Linger, experience them, always with calm reflective self talk.

Objects

Meditate on objects, hard or soft, warm or cold, large or small, fixed or moving, their touch and feel. A rose is a good object since it has a hard stem, soft petals, sharp thorns, and a pleasant fragrance. It has been an effective meditative object for thousands of years. Any object can be used. In time you can choose objects at random "to be one with." This helps you open your mind's eye.

Feelings

Feelings can also be used as the subject for meditation: pleasant or unpleasant, fixed, changing, or mixed. Observe how feelings arise and change, how they come and go and fade, how they change, how they pass over and through you as clouds pass over the earth.

MINDFULNESS

Mind meditation is like observing someone else's thinking. Ernest Hilgard, professor of psychology at Stanford University, described it as "a hidden observer." Meditate on whatever is in your mind, from the trivial to the serious. Some of what your mind conjures up will bring a smile! You will begin to see how foolish some thoughts are. Mind meditation is important for that reason. It helps you first to see what is there and then sort out what's really important. Buddha recommended dwelling on deeper thoughts such as good (what is it?), the absence of good, lust and its absence, thinking and feeling (which is better?), form and formlessness, simplicity and complexity, selfishness and selflessness, serenity and stress. Doing this opens the door to deeper meditation.

NOW AND ZEN

Applying Zen thinking can become a useful springboard to higher meditative awareness. To develop this ability, reflect on the koans and parables in Chapter 3. Think of more than one answer to the koans and remember that the object is satori, the flash of mystic light, not facts or logic. When this way of thinking becomes automatic or within easy reach in your everyday life it will enrich and broaden the scope of your meditative awareness.

Another way to use Zen thinking is to stop whatever you're doing from time to time and let whatever is happening happen, doing nothing yourself. Often things, thoughts, and feelings you were not aware of come to your attention at these moments. Flowers and birdsong, blue sky and clouds, sound and silence, still and moving air, something and nothing can be among life's most moving moments.

✳ | References

Arnold, Edward. *The Light of Asia*. Boston: Roberts Brothers, 1897.

Beck, Emily, ed. *Familiar Quotations by John Bartlett*. Boston: Little, Brown and Company, 1968.

Beilenson, Peter, ed. and trans. *Japanese Haiku*. Mount Vernon, New York: Peter Pauper Press, 1956.

Bodhi, Bhikku. *The Noble Eightfold Path*. Kandy, Sri Lanka: Buddhist Publication Society, 1984.

Buchanan, Daniel, ed. and trans. *One Hundred Famous Haiku*. San Francisco: Japan Publications, 1973.

Campbell, Joseph. *Oriental Mythology*. Masks of God series. New York: Viking Penguin, 1976.

Camphausen, Rufus. *The Divine Library*. Rochester, VT: Inner Traditions International, 1992.

Coleman, Graham, trans. *The Tibetan Book of the Dead*. New York: Viking, 2005.

Dhammapada, the Buddha's Path to Wisdom. Kandy, Sri Lanka: Buddhist Publication Society, n.d.

Emerson, Ralph. *Essays of Ralph Waldo Emerson*. Garden City, NY: Halcyon House, 1941.

Evans-Wentz, W. Y. *The Tibetan Book of the Dead*. New York: Oxford University Press, 2000.

Halevi, Z'Ev Ben Shimon. *Kabbalah, Tradition of Hidden Meaning*. New York: Thames and Hudson, 1979.

Hume, Robert, trans. *The Upanishads*. Petaluma, CA: Nilgiri Press, 1985.

Ingbert-Gruttner, Jean Le Mee, trans. *Hymns from the Rig Veda*. New York: Random House, 1975.

Kaltenmark, Max, and Roger Greaves. *Lao Tzu and Taoism*. Stanford: Stanford University Press, 1965.

Kapleau, Paul. *Three Pillars of Zen.* Boston: Beacon Press, 1965.

Krishnamurti, Jiddu. *Think on These Things.* San Francisco: Harper Collins, 1975.

———. *Meditations.* San Francisco: Harper Collins, 1979.

Lao Tse. *The Book of Lao Tzu, the Tao Te Ching.* Translated by Yi Wu. San Francisco: Great Learning, 1989.

———. *The Book of Tao.* Translated by Frank MacHovec. White Plains, NY: Peter Pauper, 1962.

———. *The Canon of Reason and Virtue, Being Lao-Tzu's Tao Teh King.* Translated by Paul Carus. Chicago: Open Court, 1913.

———. *Lao-Tzu Te-Tao Ching: A New Translation Based on the Recently Discovered Ma-wang-tui Texts.* Translated by Robert Henricks. New York: Ballantine, 1989.

———. *Lao-Tse Tao Te King.* Translated by Victor Strauss. Zurich: Manesee Verlag, 1959.

———. *Lao Tzu: Text, Notes, and Comments.* Translated by Ku-Ying Ch'en. Beijing: Chinese Materials Center, 1981.

———. *The Sayings of Lao Tzu.* Translated by Lionel Giles. 1905.

———. *Taoism, the Road to Immortality.* Translated by John Blofeld. Boulder: Shambhala Publications, 1958.

———. *Taoist Teachings from the Book of Lieh Tzu.* Translated by Lionel Giles. London: John Murray, 1912.

———. *The Tao of Power: A Translation of the Tao Te Ching by Lao Tzu.* Translated by R. L. Wing. Garden City, NY: Doubleday Dolphin, 1986.

———. *Tao of the Tao Te Ching: A Translation and Commentary.* Translated by Michael LaFargue. Albany, NY: State University of New York Press, 1992.

———. *Tao Te Ching: A New English Version.* Translated by Stephen Mitchell. New York: Harper and Row, 1988.

———. *Tao Te Ching: The Book of the Way and Its Virtue.* Translated by J. J. L. Duyvendak. London: John Murray, 1954.

———. *Tao Te Ching.* Translated by D. C. Lau. Baltimore: Penguin, 1963.

———. *Tao Te Ching.* Translated by Gia-Fu Feng and Jane English. New York: Alfred A. Knopf, 1972.

———. *Tao Te Ching.* Translated by Ta-Kao Ch'u. Cambridge: Cambridge University Press, 1937.

———. *Tao Te Ching.* Translated by Victor Mair. New York: Bantam Books, 1990.

————. *The Tao Te Ching.* Translated by Wing-tsit Chan. New York: Samuel Weiser, 1963.

————. *Tao Teh Ching.* Translated by John Wu. New York: Barnes and Noble, 1961.

————. *Tao Teh King Interpreted as Nature and Intelligence.* 1958. Reprint. Translated by Archie Bahm. New York: Frederick Ungar, 1970.

————. *Tao: The Watercourse Way.* Translated by Alan Watts. New York: Pantheon, 1975.

————. *The Teachings of Lao Tzu: The Tao-Te Ching.* Translated by Paul Carus. 1898. Reprint. New York: St. Martin's Press, 2000.

————. *The Way and Its Power: A Study of the Tao Te-Ching and Its Place in Chinese Thought.* Translated by Arthur Waley. London: Allen and Unwin, 1934.

————. *The Way of Life According to Lao Tzu.* Translated by Witter Bynner. New York: Putnam, 1944.

————. *The Way of Life, Tao Te Ching.* Translated by Raymond Blakney. 1905. Reprint. New York: Mentor, 1955.

————. *The Wisdom of Lao Tse.* Translated by Lin Yutang. New York: Random House, 1948.

Legge, James, trans. *The Sacred Books of China: The Texts of Taoism.* Oxford: Oxford University Press, 1885.

Littleton, Scott. *Shinto: Origins, Rituals, Spirits, and Sacred Places.* New York: Oxford University Press, 2002.

MacHovec, Frank, trans. *I Ching: The Book of Changes.* White Plains NY: Peter Pauper Press, 1971.

————, trans. *The Tibetan Book of the Dead.* White Plains, NY: Peter Pauper Press, 1973.

————. *Yoga: Guide to Inner Tranquility.* White Plains, NY: Peter Pauper Press, 1973.

————. *Spiritual Intelligence, the Behavioral Sciences and the Humanities.* Lewiston, NY: Edwin Mellen, 2002.

Maslow, Abraham. *The Farther Reaches of Human Nature.* New York: Viking, 1971.

Mendis, N. K. G., trans. *The Questions of King Milinda.* Kandy, Sri Lanka: Buddhist Publication Society, 1973.

Merton, Thomas. *Mystics and Zen Masters.* New York: Dell, 1968.

Miyamoto, Musashi. *The Book of Five Rings.* Translated by Victor Harris. New York: Overlook Press, 1982.

————. *The Way of Victory: The Annotated Book of Five Rings.* Translated by Hidy Ochiai. New York: Overlook Press, 2001.

Mukerji, Dhan Gopal, trans. *The Song of God: Translation of the Bhagavad Gita.* New York: E. P. Dutton, 1929.

Myokyo-Ni and Ramiah, L. S., trans. *Gentling the Bull: The Ten Bull Pictures, a Spiritual Journey.* New York: Tuttle Publishing, 1996.

Naranjo, Claudio. *The Healing Journey: New Approaches to Consciousness.* New York: Pantheon, 1973.

Picken, Stuart. *Shinto, Japan's Spiritual Roots.* Tokyo and New York: Kodansha International, 1980.

Rinpoche, Sogyal, trans. The *Tibetan Book of the Dead.* San Francisco: Harper Collins, 1994.

Scholem, Gershom. *Kabbalah.* New York: Dorset Press, 1974.

Sokyo, Ono. *Shinto: The Kami Way.* New York: Tuttle Publishing, 1994.

Thurman, Robert, trans. *The Tibetan Book of the Dead.* New York: Bantam Books, 1993.

Waddell, Norman, trans. *The Life of Kakuin: Life Records of the Japanese Zen Master.* New York: Kodansha America, 1995.

Waley, Arthur, trans. *The Analects of Confucius.* London: Allen and Unwin, 1938.

Welch, Holmes. *Taoism: The Parting of the Way.* Boston: Beacon Press, 1957.

Wilhelm, Richard, trans. *I Ching or the Book of Changes.* Princeton: Princeton University Press, 1967.

✳ | Index

Chu Hsi, 133

Confucius. *See* K'ung FuTse

Creation force (Ch'ien; *I Ching*), 79

Daughter force (*I Ching*): first (Sun), second (Li), third (Tui), 79

Dead Sea Scrolls, 17

Defilements (Buddha), 30

Delphi, Oracle of, 18

Dhamma (Dharma), 19, 21–22, 34

Dharana, 116–17

Diamond vehicle (Buddha), 22

Dogen, 35

Dukkha, 25

Durga, 23, 104

Dhyana, 36, 117–18

Earth force (K'un; *I Ching*), 79

East-West compared, 13–14, 159

Eight limbs of yoga, 106, 109–22

Eightfold Path (Buddha), 25, 27

Eisai, 35

Emerson, 127

Enlightenment, 11–12, 16–17, 21–23, 25, 27, 31, 38, 43, 45, 58, 62, 70, 99, 101, 119, 133, 135–36, 139, 150, 152–54, 157–58

Eros libido, 23–24, 104–5

Essenes, 17

Existentialism, 47

Falun Gong, Falun Dafa, 134–35

Father force (Ch'ien; *I Ching*), 79. *See also* Yin-Yang

Feng Shui: 130; compass school, 133; magic square, 131–32; principles school, 133; shapes

and forms, 132–33

Fire force (Li; *I Ching*), 79

Five abstinences, 109

Five elements (Feng Shui), 130–31

Five precepts (Buddha), 22

Five Rings (Musashi), 142–48

Flag of India, 25

Flag of South Korea, 130

Four Noble Truths (Buddha), 25–27

Freud, 23, 104

Fromm, 15

Fu Hsi, 78–79

Gandhi, 18, 107

Gautama Siddhartha. *See* Buddhism

Gnostic Christians, 17

Goleman, 15

Gorinsho (Shinto), 142

Great Enlightenment (Buddha), 21

Great Renunciation (Buddha), 21

Greek Asklepian temples, 29, 159

Green dragon (Feng Shui), 132–33

Guna, 120

Guru, 109

Gyana yoga, 107

Haiku, 148–50

Hassidic Jews, 17

Hatha yoga, 107–8

Heaven force (Ch'ien; *I Ching*), 79

Heraclitus of Ephesus, 18

Hilgard, 165

Himalayas, 50

Hinayana Buddhism, 22, 35–36, 150

Hinduism: 23–25; gods, literature, 104–6; Sikhs, 17

Index

173

STONE
BRIDGE
PRESS

OTHER TITLES OF INTEREST
FROM STONE BRIDGE PRESS

All titles available at bookstores worldwide and online. For more information, visit www.stonebridge.com.